THE GOLDEN BOOK
KRAKOW

Text by
GRZEGORZ RUDZIŃSKI

BONECHI-GALAKTYKA

Project and editorial conception:
Casa Editrice Bonechi
Publication Manager:
Monica Bonechi
Picture research:
Sonia Gottardo
*Graphic design, make-up
and cover:*
Sonia Gottardo
Text by
Grzegorz Rudziński
Translation:
Heather MacKay Roberts,
Eve Leckey
Drawings:
Stefano Benini

© Copyright
by Casa Editrice Bonechi,
Florence - Italy
E-mail: bonechi@bonechi.it

Printed in Italy by Centro
Stampa Editoriale Bonechi.

*The photographs are the property
of* Casa Editrice Bonechi
Archives and were taken by
Marco Bonechi, Maria Novella
Batini *and* Andrea Pistolesi.

Other contributors:
Press Photo:
page 114;
Associated Press:
pages 117 (photo by Ron Frehm);
Jan Włodarczyk/BE&W:
page 127.

*The publisher will be grateful
for information concerning the
sources of photographs without
credits and will be pleased
to acknoledge them in future
editions.*

ISBN 978-88-476-2075-9
www.bonechi.com

A 10 9 8 7 6 5 4 3 2 1

HISTORY

THE ORIGINS

200.000 B.C.	Earliest settlements in the area of Krakow
50.000 B.C.	Earliest settlements in the area of the Wawel hill
1st C. A.D.	First contacts with the Roman Empire
8th Century	Krakow capital of the Vistulan State
9th Century	Krakow temporarily absorbed by the Empire of Great Moravia

MIDDLE AGES AND RENAISSANCE

1000	Diocese of Krakow comes into being
1038	Krakow capital of Poland
1079	Martyrdom of Bishop Stanislaw
12th Century	Duchy of Krakow created
13th Century	Urban development of the city following devastating attacks by the Tartars; defensive walls are built around the city
14th-15th C.	Numerous churches are built and the Cathedral is greatly restructured
1364	University of Krakow is founded
16th Century	Royal Castle of Wawel is rebuilt
1596	Royal court moves from Krakow to Warsaw

MODERN AGE

1609	Sigismund III transfers the capital to Warsaw
17th Century	The city goes into a state of decline
1655-1657	Krakow occupied first by Swedish troops and then by the Transylvanian army
1702-1718	The city is invaded alternately by the Swedes and the Russians
1734	The king is crowned in Krakow for the last time
End of 18th C.	Krakow becomes part of the Austrian province of Galicia
1809	The city is annexed to the Duchy of Warsaw
1815	The independent Republic of Krakow is recognised
1846	After the failure of the uprising, Krakow is annexed to Austria but from 1866 enjoys considerable autonomy

20th CENTURY

1914-1918	During the First World War Krakowian troops fight for the liberation of Poland
1918-1939	Development of the city: AGH University of Science and Technology (1919); radio station (1926); Wawel – restoration work in progress
1939-1945	Nazi occupation: mass arrest of scholars; theft of cultural possessions; massacre of the jews
1949	Beginning of construction work in Nowa Huta
1978	The historic centre of the city is added to the first UNESCO world heritage list

Krakow – the cultural capital of Poland

"Krakow was not built in a day", claims an old Polish proverb referring to an outstanding feature of this city - its extremely long history. For centuries the capital of Poland, and an important centre on the European panorama, the city has ancient origins. From the 14th century it was home to a prestigious university and is now considered to be the nation's cultural capital.

ORIGINS

Krakow developed over thousands rather than hundreds of years. Temporary settlements by nomads in the Palaeolithic period were followed by more permanent ones some five thousand years ago. Remains of the earliest settlements have been found on the Wawel hill, which was to become the political centre of the community. Archaeological excavations bear witness to the uninterrupted local production of objects, from the tools of the Neolithic period to later pieces in bronze and iron. The **mining** of metals began in the area about 1700 B.C. Numerous objects from the Roman period (1st-4th centuries A.D.) reflect the lively commercial relationship between Krakow and the Empire. The oldest monument in Krakow dates to the 7th century and is a mound some 16 metres high known as the **Krak Tumulus**.

ANCIENT KRAKOW

We can trace the beginnings of the Vistulan when a small fortified city (gród), with (podgrodzie), was built on the Wawel hill. In the 10th centuries Krakow came under the influence and then of Bohemia. It is to this period that we ment relating to Krakow, in which the name of Arabic by a certain Ibrahim Ibn-Yaqub (a Jewish can be interpreted as **Karako** or **Krakua**. In the riage was celebrated between the Bohemian and duke **Mieszko** of the Piast dynasty - founders of Poland - leader of the Polans Gniezno, capital of Great Poland. This un- Krakow's future relations with Poland. converted to Christianity, Poland be- the traditional Roman Christian culture. death Mieszko took possession of the "State gave it to his son Bolesław the Brave, who unit- (known since that time as Lesser Poland) Poland and then established a unified

state to the 8th century surrounding towns course of the 9th and first of Greater Moravia date the earliest docu- the city, transcribed in merchant from Spain), same year 965 the mar- princess Dobrava recognised as the and resident in ion determined When Mieszko came part of After Dobrava's of Krakow" and ed this territory with Great monarchy.

KRAKOW - CAPITAL OF POLAND

In 1000 Krakow became an **episcopal** fore gained importance over other Polish duke **Casimir the Restorer** established administration in Krakow thus making it capital of his vast dominions. It was in Kra- than in Gniezno in 1076 that Bolesław

see and there- cities. In 1038 his central effectively the kow rather the Bold

Seen here are the lofty towers of the Church of the Virgin Mary.

was consecrated King of Poland, and his successor Władysław Herman minted coins bearing the name of **Krakow**.

What sort of city was Krakow at that time? The **romanesque Cathedral**, the **Royal Castle** built of stone and the wood and stone citadel surrounded by ramparts were all built on the hill of Wawel. To the north of the hill **Okół** continued to expand, a completely independent city with fortified walls, containing the romanesque churches dedicated to St Gilles and St Andrew.

The breakdown of the Polish territory into small feudal duchies marked a period of continuous unrest but also of steady progress in Krakow. Germanic colonies began to penetrate vast areas of sparsely populated Polish territory and when, in 1241, the Tartar armies invaded southern Poland, Krakow suffered serious damage. The accession to power in 1243 of Bolesław the Bashful, who reigned in Lesser Poland for some 36 years, marked the beginning of a period of peace and continued development. On 6 June 1257 the Duke conferred the "privilege of location" on the city, bringing an end to the period of its early history.

The 13th century witnessed the emergence of **gothic Krakow** with buildings built of brick in contrast to the earlier, mainly stone, romanesque architecture, and it is the city's gothic character which still prevails today.

In 1287 when Krakow was threatened by renewed attacks from invading Tartar armies, the **strong walls** which had been built around the city protected it from destruction by the barbarians. On the verge of the 13th and 14th century the city was the scene of the struggle for the restoration of the Polish kingdom. The crown finally returned to the **Piast** dynasty when in 1320 Ladislaus the Short was crowned in Wawel Cathedral where he was to be buried in 1333. He was the first of the Polish kings to be buried there; the building became the royal burial place and Krakow the official capital of Poland.

THE GOLDEN AGE

The accession to the throne of **Casimir the Great** (1333-70), the last sovereign of the Piast dynasty, marks the beginning of Krakow's ascendancy which lasted over 200 years. Casimir the Great founded the

University in 1364, and built a fortified city on the other side of the Vistula, **Kazimierz**, which eventually became absorbed by Krakow. He promoted the textile industry and encouraged local trade. The marriage of his niece, Jadwiga, to the Lithuanian Grand-duke, Jagiełło, signalled the rise of a new dynasty (Jagiellon) in the Polish kingdom. Governed by the **Jagiellons**, Poland enjoyed a period of great military strength and economic prosperity. In 1410 Jagiellon, together with his brother Vitoldo, did much to free Poland from the oppressive power of the Teutonic order. Under Casimir IV (1447-92) Poland regained control over access to the Baltic and, as a result of a dispute with Moldavia, recovered the ports on the Black Sea. There was considerable commercial expansion in the Polish cities and Krakow was among those which increased in size and prosperity.

In the second half of the 15th century the Academy at Krakow attracted students from all over Central Europe, including **Nicholas Copernicus** from 1491 to 1495. By the early 16th century interest in the humanist movement and the Renaissance brought about what later became known as "the golden age of Polish culture". In 1525 in Rynek Główny, the Market Square of Krakow, Albrecht Hohenzollern, last Grand Master of the Teutonic Order and the first duke of Prussia, paid homage to King Sigismund I in recognition of his supremacy. Sigismund had the Royal Castle on **Wawel hill** rebuilt in the Italian renaissance style, thus creating one of the finest monuments in that style north of the Alps. Krakow was a lively

centre at the time and high offices could be obtained by men of various nationalities - Poles, Germans, Jews, Italians, Hungarians - no matter what their social background. In the late 16th and early 17th centuries Sigismund III Vasa (1587-1632) involved the country in wars to the north, and the capital was transferred from Krakow to Warsaw. Krakow retained much of its ancient prestige and the Cathedral remained the site of the coronation of the Polish kings but during the two wars with Sweden (1655-60 and 1703-21) the city suffered much damage. After the second Partition, **Tadeusz Kościuszko** determined to safeguard what remained of Polish sovereignty, and on 24 March 1794 in Krakow he proclaimed a national insurrection, but the Prussians sacked Krakow and carried off the royal treasure from the Castle of Wawel.

THE 19TH AND 20TH CENTURIES

*T*he city remained unscathed during the Napoleonic campaign, and the Congress of Vienna (1815) instituted the Republic of Krakow. Throughout the 19th century the city played a leading role in Polish artistic and cultural life. The University slowly regained its prestige; Karol Olszewski and Zygmunt Wróblewski were the first to succeed in distilling oxygen and nitrogen from liquefied air. In 1879 the National Museum was founded to house paintings and sculptures by Polish artists, including the monumental works of **Jan Matejko**, while the **Czartoryski Museum** displays important works of art. During the tragic period of Nazi occupation the Jewish population of Krakow, a community which had enriched the history of the city for centuries, was totally exterminated. In 1978 Krakow was included on the UNESCO list of the twelve most remarkable architectural sites in the world. The same year saw the election of the city's archbishop **Karol Wojtyła** as Pope John Paul II.

The façades of the elegant buildings surrounding Market Square, the heart of the city.

STARE MIASTO
Old Town

RYNEK GŁÓWNY
The Market Square

The 13th-century layout of Krakow has survived unaltered since the city was founded, to the present day. Rynek Główny is one of the largest medieval squares in Europe. A slightly irregular quadrangle some 200 metres on each side, the surrounding houses were built in the 14th and 15th centuries.

The classical façades on a large number of the houses were the result of restoration work carried out from the 17th to the 19th centuries but many retain renaissance and baroque stone doorways, together with many other original architectural details such as the beams, porticoed courtyards and sections of the attic storeys. Among the most notable buildings on the square are the **Sukiennice** (Textile Warehouse), **Wieża Ratuszowa** (Town Hall Tower), **Kościół św. Wojciecha** (the Church of St Adalbert), the **Zbaraskich Palace** (at no. 20), the **monument to Adam Mickiewicz**, and especially **Kościół Mariacki** (Church of the Virgin Mary). The present level of the square, paved with stone slabs, is some two metres higher than originally, as we can see from the lower part of the wall on the south side of the Church of the Virgin Mary and also from the sunken level of the Church of St Adalbert.

A visit to Rynek Główny not only gives us a chance to admire its architectural beauty and understand something of the city's history but also provides a pleasant pause for shopping and relaxing in the numerous cafés, restaurants and shops that surround it.

Outside the Church of St Adalbert on the south corner of the Sukiennice among the paving stones is a marble slab indicating the site where Albrecht Hohenzollern, Grand Master of the Teutonic Order, paid tribute to the King of Poland thus recognising his supremacy. Not far from the Town Hall Tower, at no. 30, is another slab commemorating the oath made by Tadeusz Kościuszko. In the palace at no. 7, **Kamienica Montelupich**, the first Polish post-office was installed in 1558. At no. 13 is a chemist's which has been there since 1403. The square also houses the most famous Polish cabaret in **"Piwnica pod Baranami"** ("Cellar of the Rams"). There are four permanent exhibitions in Rynek Główny: in the Sukiennice is a section of the **Galeria Sztuki Polskiej XIX wieku** (Gallery of 19th-Century Polish Art); the basement of the Church of St Adalbert houses part of the **Muzeum Archeologiczne w Krakowie** (Archaeological Museum); lastly, the Krzysztofory Palace (Rynek Główny, 35) and the Town Hall Tower include two exhibitions from the **Muzeum Historyczne Miasta Krakowa** (Museum of the History of Krakow).

Aerial view of Market Square with the Textile Warehouse at the centre, flanked by the Town Hall Tower and the Church of the Virgin Mary in the background.

Rynek Główny

Boner House
The top storey of the Boner Palace (no. 9 Rynek Główny) is over eight metres high. On the lower level of the façade are three statues of hermaphrodites. These are surmounted by two masks of satyrs and four griffins intertwined; crowning these are three stone balls.

Wierzynek Restaurant
is the oldest restaurant in Krakow. The dining rooms have fine renaissance ceilings.

Hetman's House dates from the 14th century. The ground floor has gothic cross vaults bearing the arms of the regions of Poland on the intersecting bosses. The gothic door and portal were re-discovered in 1979.

The **Dom Pod Obrazem (Madonna House)** takes its name from the image of the Madonna painted on the facade in 1718.

Dating from 1773, the **Poto... Palace** has a neoclassical fac... with allegorical figures. The building is a fine example classical Krakow town hous...

KOŚCIÓŁ ŚW. WOJCIECHA (The Church of St Adalbert)

UL. GRODZKA

UL. BRACKA

Kamienica Pod Jaszczurami (Lizards' House);
takes its name from the coat of arms on the façade (the original plaque is in the National Museum).

Montelupi House originally a gothic building but rebuilt in the renaissance style in 1556. The Montelupi family were from Florence and were responsible for organizing Poland's first postal service in the 16th century as recalled by the commemorative plaque.

EAST SIDE

Kamienica Szara (Grey House)
dating from the late 13th-early 14th centuries, this is the oldest burgher's house in the town. The interior has both gothic vaults and renaissance ceilings.

4 Market Square

KOŚCIÓŁ ŚW. BARBARY (The Church of St Barbara)

PLAC MARIACKI (St Mary's Square)

A **passage** links Mały Rynek with Plac Mariacki

MAŁY RYNEK (Small Market Square)

MAŁY RYNEK, medieval buil...

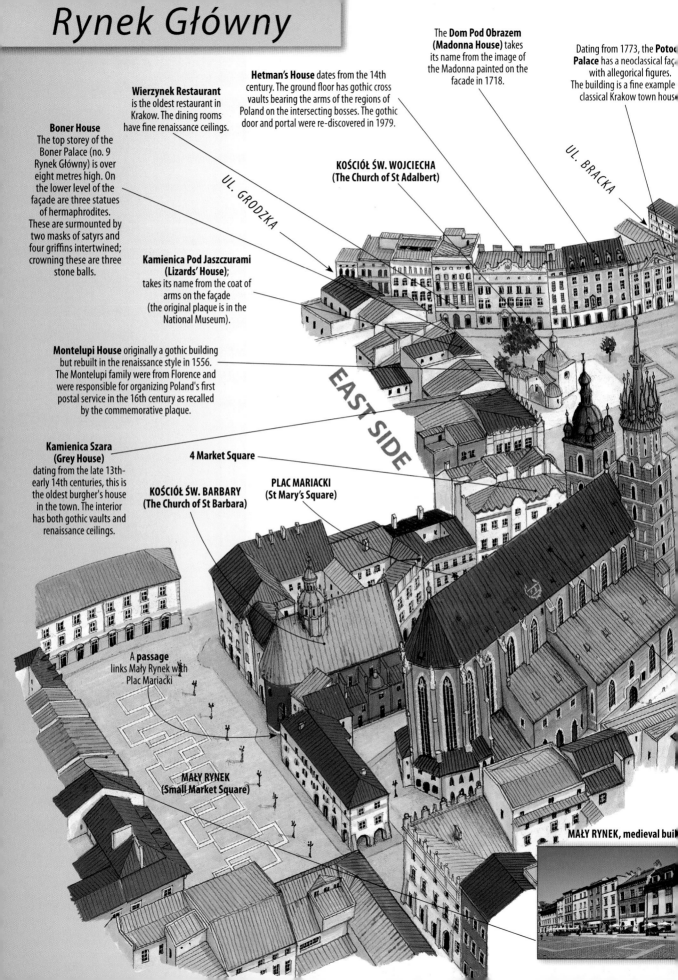

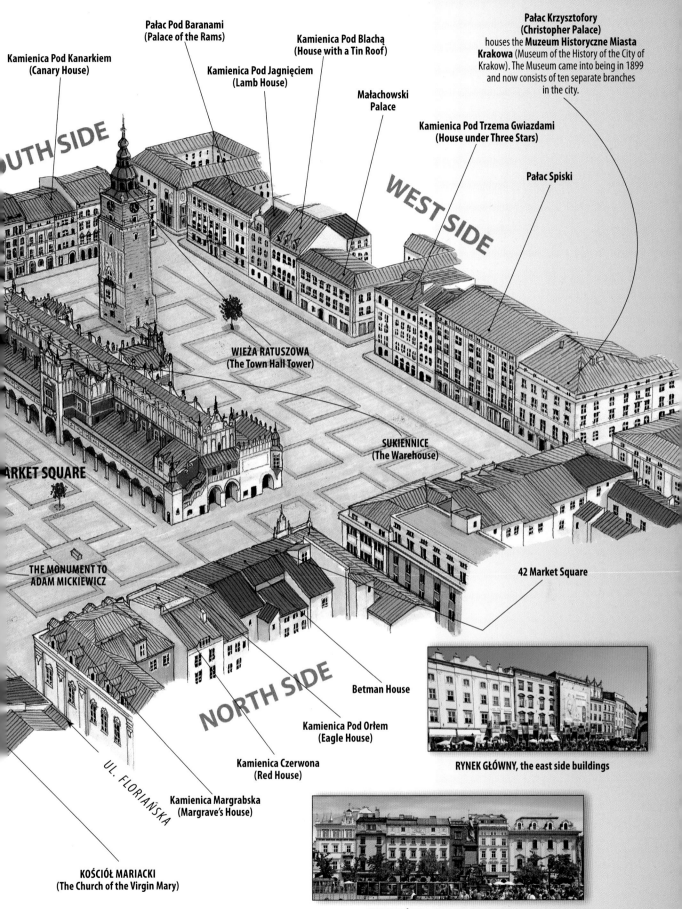

Kamienica Pod Kanarkiem
(Canary House)

Pałac Pod Baranami
(Palace of the Rams)

Kamienica Pod Jagnięciem
(Lamb House)

Kamienica Pod Blachą
(House with a Tin Roof)

Małachowski
Palace

Kamienica Pod Trzema Gwiazdami
(House under Three Stars)

Pałac Spiski

Pałac Krzysztofory
(Christopher Palace)
houses the **Muzeum Historyczne Miasta Krakowa** (Museum of the History of the City of Krakow). The Museum came into being in 1899 and now consists of ten separate branches in the city.

OUTH SIDE

WEST SIDE

WIEŻA RATUSZOWA
(The Town Hall Tower)

SUKIENNICE
(The Warehouse)

ARKET SQUARE

THE MONUMENT TO
ADAM MICKIEWICZ

42 Market Square

NORTH SIDE

Betman House

Kamienica Pod Orłem
(Eagle House)

Kamienica Czerwona
(Red House)

UL. FLORIAŃSKA

Kamienica Margrabska
(Margrave's House)

RYNEK GŁÓWNY, the east side buildings

KOŚCIÓŁ MARIACKI
(The Church of the Virgin Mary)

RYNEK GŁÓWNY, the north side buildings

The Colourful Life of the Market Square

Rynek Główny is not only the old medieval centre of the town, surrounded by museums, galleries and unique and beautiful buildings. This extensive square is also lively with street artists, cafes, restaurants and clubs; traditional events take place here and the flowers of which Krakowians are so fond are sold from stalls. The statue to Adam Mickiewicz is a popular meeting place for Krakowians – and the swooping pigeons too. Rynek Główny is alive with bright colours yet it is also the elegant heart of the city, stylish and sophisticated, where relaxed and friendly entertainment of all kinds is to be found. Temporary exhibitions attract tourists who are often tempted to buy original works.

The main cultural and artistic centre of Poland, a major university city with 150,000 students, without any doubt Krakow is a lively and creative city in every sense, full of a love of life, energetic and embracing the future while carefully respecting tradition.

Krakow is the main international tourist centre of Poland and the visitor who really wants to get to know the city will absorb its bubbling and youthful atmosphere and discover its true character not only by appreciating the monuments, but also visiting the cafes, restaurants, parks, unusual little corners and especially getting acquainted with its delightful inhabitants.

SUKIENNICE
The Textile Warehouse

The Sukiennice (Warehouse) stands right in the middle Market Square, with its extremities at the north and south ends. Both the east and west façades are 100 metres long and extend symmetrically on either side of the entrances. The **arcades** with their neo-gothic ogival arches give rhythm and focus to the lower part of the building. The **capitals** deserve attention as each single one is different. The roof above the arcades has a stone **neo-gothic balustrade** and the attic floor above is decorated with **masks**. There are external staircases at both ends of the building, covered with coffered ceilings; the one at the north end is particularly fine.

Inside the building, the ground floor is full of wooden stalls and **shops** selling local crafts. Amateur artists display their works in the transept. The upper floor, reached from the staircase beside the main entrance, houses part of the National Museum in Krakow, the **Gallery of 19th-Century Polish Art**. However today the Gallery has been moved to the Castle in Niepołomice and will stay there until 2010.

Previous pages: the most popular transport in Krakow Old Town with the Sukiennice and Town Hall Tower in the background.

A detail of the balcony over the eastern entrance, with Krakow's coat of arms representing the royal crown surmounting a section of the city walls with three towers and an open door framing an eagle with its wings spread.

The Warehouse has been enlarged and altered over several periods, from the very earliest – when Krakow received the status of a city in 1257 – to the present day. The original building dates from the reign of Casimir the Great who in 1358 ordered the construction of a large covered brick market, 100 metres long. Entrance to the building was through two large ogival doorways, one each in the middle of the two main façades leading into the building. In the 16th century the renaissance-style attic storey was added to the original structure and the building was further decorated with masks attributed to the Florentine Santi Gucci; Giovanni Maria Mosca, called il Padovano, divided the Sukiennice horizontally and built the staircase at the end of the building to unite the two floors. The last large-scale reconstruction of the building was between 1875 and 1879 when Tomasz Pryliński added the neo-gothic arcade with capitals on the columns designed by Jan Matejko (1838-93).

THE MONUMENT TO ADAM MICKIEWICZ

The monument to the greatest Polish romantic poet, Adam Mickiewicz, who was born in Lithuania in 1798 and died in Istanbul in 1855, was erected at the end of the 19th century to mark the return of his ashes, now in Wawel Cathedral. Designed by Teodor Rygier (1841-1919) the statue stands on a high pedestal, its sides covered with allegorical figures. The front of the pedestal shows the *Homeland* depicted as a young woman raising her arm with the figure of *Poetry* on her left, holding a lute. The elderly figure teaching a boy is an allegory of *Science*, and the young knight symbolises *Patriotism*. The monument is highly academic in style and reflects the Art Nouveau movement, then in vogue. The statue is an extremely popular meeting place and on 24 December, St Adam's day, all the florists of Krakow lay flowers on the monument in memory of the great poet.

The pedestal of the monument to Adam Mickiewicz is a popular meeting place for Krakowians and tourists alike.

The monument standing in front of the Warehouse and the Town Hall Tower in the background.

Souvenirs and crafts

Traditional stalls line the portico of the lovely old Sukiennice, the ancient covered textile market, displaying colourful souvenirs, traditional costumes, painted eggs, wooden dolls, Christmas decorations and craft items. The finest

traditional crafts are the silver and amber jewelry, wooden items – especially of religious subjects – and decorated pottery. The **Traditional Crafts Fair** *is held in the square every year in September when typical products of many Polish towns and villages are displayed.*

Above, the side of the Warehouse facing south.

Opposite page, the corner turret on the north side (above left) and decorations (above right) of the loft of the Warehouse in renaissance style and the side facing west (below).

GALERIA SZTUKI POLSKIEJ XIX WIEKU W SUKIENNICACH
Gallery of 19th-Century Polish Art

On the first floor of the Sukiennice is the Gallery of 19th-Century Polish Art, the largest collection of Polish painting and sculpture of the period and one of the city's major attractions. Today it is one of the 10 branches of the National Museum in Krakow which was originally housed within the Sukiennice. The Museum came into being in 1879 as a collection of contemporary Polish art and its first acquisition was the painting of *Pochodnie Nerona*, Nero's Torches, painted by Henryk Siemiradzki (1843-1902) in Rome in 1876 and famous throughout Europe before the artist donated it to the city of Krakow.

The works in this gallery represent the classicist and pre-romantic periods of the later 18th century and the Romantic period up to Symbolism and Impressionism. This important centre is being renovated as part of the **"Nowe Sukiennice"** project, which will modernise and improve the facilities of the building. While rebuilding and restoration is taking place, the exhibits have been transferred to the Royal Castle of Niepołomice, the ancient residence of the Piast and Jagiellon dynasties.

POLISH PAINTERS

IN THE SUKIENNICE COLLECTION

The historical paintings of Jan Matejko (1838-93) - including the famous *Hołd pruski,* Prussian Homage (1882) - are typically Polish in style. The Krakowian artistic movement known as "Young Poland" is well represented in the Sukiennice collection. The works of Józef Chełmoński (1849-1914) are represented by the large painting *Czwórka,* The Chariot (1881). The Polish school of Munich is also present with works by Adam Chmielowski, Józef Brandt and the Gierymski brothers. In Ulica Floriańska at no. 41 is the **housemuseum of Jan Matejko**, a Krakowian artist who is considered to be one of the leaders of Polish cultural re-awakening.

The arcades of the two symmetrical shorter sides lead into the covered market where colourful Polish craft items are displayed on the wooden stalls.

WIEŻA RATUSZOWA
The Town Hall Tower

The tower is all that remains of Krakow's old town hall, demolished in the early 19th century. The original appearance of the building can be seen in Teodor B. Stachowicz's painting *City Hall View* (1840), Museum of the History of Krakow, Christopher Palace.

The surviving tower was built in 1383 in brick with stone facing and mouldings. It has a square plan and is more than seventy metres high with a slight inclination, some fifty-five centimetres out of true. In the 18th century it was enhanced with a baroque spire. The ground floor houses a section of the **Muzeum Historyczne Miasta Krakowa** (Museum of the History of Krakow) with a unique collection of stone mason's characters and marks dating from 1444. The gothic rooms with their cross vaulted ceilings on the first floor are quite beautiful. The gallery at the top of the tower affords fine views of the Old Town.

Two views of the Town Hall Tower and the interior with an exhibition of period costumes.

KOŚCIÓŁ ŚW. WOJCIECHA
The Church of St Adalbert

This church of romanesque origin is dedicated to **St Adalbert**, the foremost patron saint of Poland and first Polish saint, a famous preacher from Prague, killed by the pagan Prussians. During his papal visit in 1997 John Paul II celebrated mass at the saint's tomb in Gniezno, a thousand years after his martyrdom.

The church stands at the corner of Ulica Grodzka and is the oldest building in the area around the Market Square. It was built between the 11th and 12th centuries and its limestone walls pre-date the *locatio civitatis* of Krakow (1257). Built on an important trade route between Hungary and Masovia, the church also played a defensive role in the protection of the Wawel citadel to the north. In 1257 it reverted to being a strictly religious building when, with the foundation of the city, it became part of a

Two views of St Adalbert's Church, the oldest building on Market Square.

Opposite, two views of the baroque interior of St Adalbert's Church and below, the romanesque foundations where the Market Square Museum is housed.

complex of buildings in and around Rynek Główny. Over the centuries the level of the square became progressively higher. Today the original level of the church entrance is two metres lower than the actual pavement level. In the 14th century the walls of the church were raised and in the 17th century the construction was totally transformed. It was during this period that the church was given its baroque decoration and the sacristy was built. The dome, covered in metal and crowned with a lantern, was built in 1611.

In the 13th and 14th centuries German-speaking population constituted the majority of Krakow's middle class. The Polish identity of the city's population became stronger during the 15th century and the German preachers were slowly moved from the major city churches to less important ones. The parish church of St Adalbert was one of the last to abandon German in the 16th century.

THE FOUNDATIONS

The 11th-century foundations in the crypt of St Adalbert's Church are particularly interesting. Excavations have revealed traces of a wooden structure, older than the early romanesque building and most probably one of the places where St Adalbert preached during his mission.

The **Market Square Museum** in the crypts houses part of Krakow's Archaeological Museum.

KOŚCIÓŁ MARIACKI
The Church of the Virgin Mary

The gothic church dedicated to the Assumption of the Virgin Mary, usually referred to as the Church of the Virgin Mary, is the most significant monument in the area of Market Square. For centuries it was the most important church in the city, frequented by the merchant classes, while the Cathedral on Wawel was officially the main diocesan church. It was built on the site of a romanesque church founded at the beginning of the 13th century by Bishop Iwo Odrowąż; now only its irregular position in relation to the plan of the Square reminds us of the earlier construction.

It is built entirely of hand-made bricks on a basilican plan with a raised central nave and two lower side aisles. The main body of the church was built between 1350 and 1397 when the architect Mikołaj Werner finished the ceiling above the central nave. It took the entire 15th century to complete the structure with the erection of the **towers**, the addition of the chapels and the completion of the ceilings.

Kościół Mariacki

THE LEGEND OF THE TWO TOWERS

The difference in height of the two towers has given rise to a legend according to which two brothers competed to see who could build the higher. The elder, when he had finished the higher north tower, murdered his brother to prevent him finishing the south tower which had almost reached the same height. He was overcome by remorse however and after confessing his crime he committed suicide by leaping from a high window of his own tower. The knife he had used to kill his brother was displayed as a sign of atonement at the entrance to the Warehouse, where it is still to be seen today.

North Tower

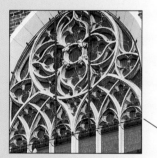

The framework of Great West Window by Jan Matejko

The main entrance, the porch

Main entrance for worshippers

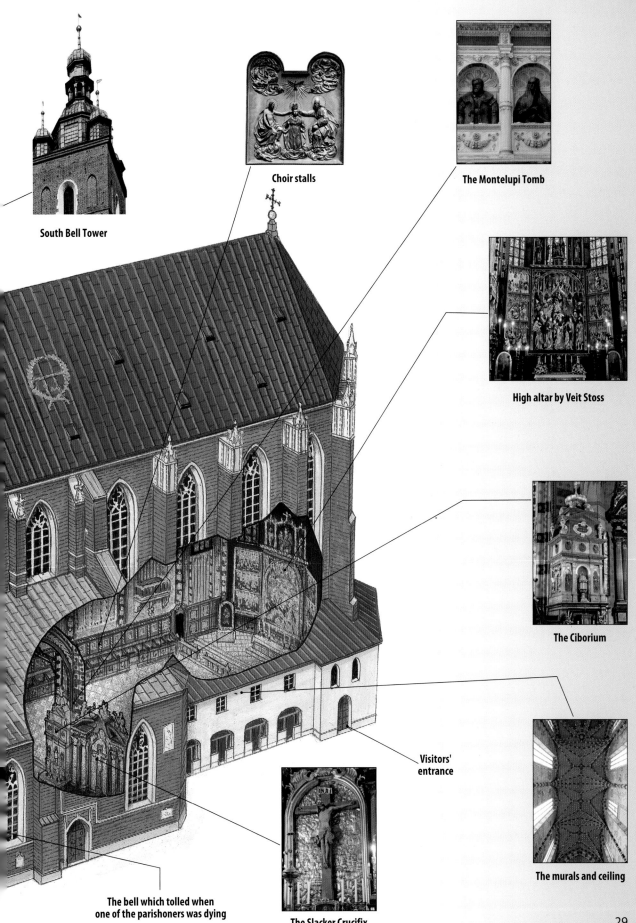

Choir stalls

The Montelupi Tomb

South Bell Tower

High altar by Veit Stoss

The Ciborium

Visitors' entrance

The murals and ceiling

The bell which tolled when
one of the parishoners was dying

The Slacker Crucifix

THE TOWERS OF KOŚCIÓŁ MARIACKI

The church towers were begun in the 15th century and, although of different heights, they were raised symmetrically from their bases. The higher north tower has eight floors of equal height while the last two floors of the lower south tower increase in height as though attempting to overtake its twin.

The **dome** on the lower tower dates from the 16th century. This tower is also the belfry and houses five bells; the largest, known as *Półzygmunt* (the half Sigismund), was cast in 1438.

The higher **gothic spire** dates from 1478 and the **golden crown**, symbol of the Virgin as Queen of Poland, was added in 1666. This tower has served as a watchtower since the Middle Ages. In the past guards were stationed there to raise the alarm in the case of fire or of attack by the enemy. Today the guards on duty must be vigilant in the prevention of fire but have also to play on the hour a musical phrase, *hejnał mariacki*. The word *hejnał* is of Hungarian origin meaning *morning* and can be interpreted as "awake", marking the hours of the day.

Opposite page, the church façade with its asymmetrical towers.

The baroque portico in front of the main entrance reserved for worshippers. The tourist entrance on the right side of the church leads directly into the splendid choir.

Right, the framework of the large stained glass window was designed by Jan Matejko. Two of the commemorative plaques along the wall of Plac Mariacki. On the centre is the plaque celebrating the victory of John III Sobieski at Vienna in 1683.

THE INTERIOR

The decoration of the church interior is in a range of styles: from the gothic to 19th-century revival, from the baroque to liberty. The most remarkable object in the church is the **altarpiece by Veit Stoss** (known in Poland as Wit Stwosz). There are also some marvellous pieces of sculpture in wood and stone from a variety of periods: crucifixes, tombs, altars. Just some of the most beautiful works here are the great gothic **stained glass windows** in the presbytery and, above the main entrance, the window designed in the late 19th century by Mehoffer, Wyspiański and Matejko who was also responsible for the decoration of the **walls** and the **vault**,

an immense undertaking, while the **choir stalls** made in 1585 are a superb example of decorative arts and carving; the **backs**, dated 1635, are decorated with quite lovely coloured biblical scenes in relief.

An impressive overview of the starry vault, the decorated walls and the nave of the Church of the Virgin Mary; at the far end is the large retablo on the main altar (12 metres high) by Veit Stoss. The gothic stained glass windows can be seen in the background.

THE ALTAR BY VEIT STOSS

The altar, a monumental wooden polyptych, is considered one of the finest pieces of European late-gothic sculpture. Carved in lime wood it is made up of a central section with four wings; the two fixed sections can only be admired when the two central mobile ones are closed. The lower part of the central panel depicts the *Dormition of the Virgin* with the Apostles while the upper section is devoted to the *Assumption*. A carved baldachin above the central panel frames the scene of the *Coronation of the Virgin* by the Holy Trinity. The mobile wings depict the *Annunciation*, the *Nativity*, the *Adoration of the Magi*,

the *Resurrection*, the *Ascension* and *Pentecost*. The predella panel is carved with the *Tree of Jesse* to show the genealogy of the Virgin. The figures in the central panel are larger than life-size, indeed the figure of St Peter supporting the body of the Virgin is 2.8 metres high.

Details of the backs of the choir stalls with beautifully coloured bas reliefs illustrating episodes from the life of the Virgin to whom the church is dedicated. Above, a royal genealogy, under the protection of the Virgin.

The Resurrection
A particularly intense detail of the Resurrection on the right side panel.

VEIT STOSS (1445 c.-1533)
The altar panel in Kościół Mariacki is perhaps the greatest masterpiece of late gothic art produced by the German sculptor, Veit Stoss, and is a work of intense spirituality. Born in Horb am Neckar, Stoss was a master wood carver, active in Krakow from 1477 to 1496; the *tomb to King Casimir IV Jagiellon* - in the Cathedral, Holy Cross Chapel - is one of the many masterpieces he created in the city. Although he continued to work in Nuremberg from 1496 until his death, his inimitable style never developed into a school in its own right.

The Assumption
A detail of the Assumption in the central panel with Christ and the Virgin Mary surrounded by a host of angels and cherubs.

The Meeting of St Anne and St Joachim.

Christ among the Doctors.

The Entombment.

The Birth of the Virgin.

The Capture of Christ.

The Descent into Hell.

The Presentation of the Virgin in the Temple.

The Crucifixion.

The three Marys at the Sepulchre.

The Ciborium
Several Italian artists worked on the basilica during the period of the Renaissance; the elaborate ciborium in classical style was commissioned from Giovanni Maria Padovano by King Sigismund the Elder.

The Montelupi Tomb
The tomb was made by the workshop of the sculptor Santi Gucci in the early 17th century for one of the richest families in Krakow, Italian merchants and bankers originally from Tuscany. Probably Florentine, Gucci completed many works for the court and his Pińczów workshop developed a mannerist style which became very popular throughout Poland.

The Slacker Crucifix
Veit Stoss made the crucifix out of a single slab of stone in 1480-90 for the court minter Henryk Slacker. The elegant silverwork panel behind was made at a later date by Józef Ceypler (1723) and represents the city of Jerusalem.

The Vault
The blue vault sprinkled with stars, a splendid fresco made by Matejko in the late 19th century, is inspired by the blue heavens seen in gothic vaults.

PLAC MARIACKI
(St Mary's Square)

Enclosed between the palaces on the east side of the adjacent Market Square and the churches of the Virgin Mary and St Barbara, St Mary's Square is built on the site of the old parish **cemetery**. The last burials took place in the 18th century. The walls of the churches of the Virgin Mary and St Barbara bear epitaphs to Krakow merchants, with inscriptions in both Latin and Polish, the earliest dating from the 16th century. A memorial plaque on one of the buildings records how Stanisław Wyspiański wrote one of his most important dramas, *Wesele* (The Wedding), when living here. Today this area has a charming and tranquil atmosphere, created by the unusual acoustics which perfectly reproduce the tune of the *hejnał*. The attractive **fountain** in the middle of the square was commissioned by the craftsmen of Krakow. The graceful figure of a melancholic young man with a turban is a perfectly proportioned piece created by the masterful skill of Veit Stoss and is a copy cast in bronze by the craftsmen of Krakow in 1958. The much smaller original is part of the frame of the main scene of the altarpiece in St Mary's Church.

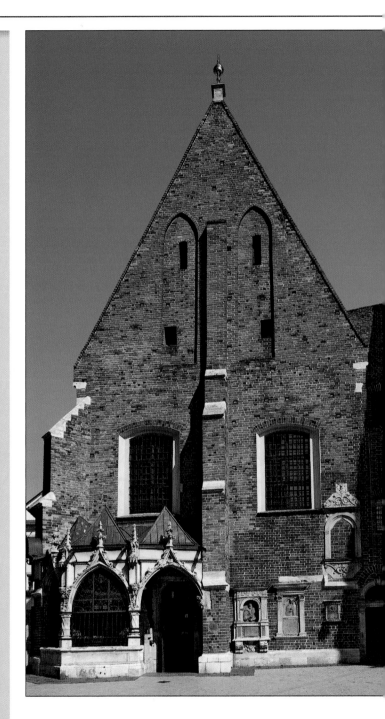

KOŚCIÓŁ ŚW. BARBARY OGRÓJEC
The Church of St Barbara and Ogrójec

Tradition has it that the Church of St Barbara, founded in 1362 by Mikołaj Wierzynek, was built with the bricks left over from the Church of the Virgin Mary. It was used as a funerary chapel. Externally, despite many renovations, the original gothic style has been preserved.

In the north wall of the church there is a memorial plaque to Jakub Wujek – the author of the remarkable translation of the Bible into Polish published in 1599.

The church **interior** is decorated according to the taste of the 17th century, when the last restoration work was carried out. The church buildings of Kościół św. Barbary separate St Mary's Square from Mały Rynek (Small Market Square) which is reached through a passageway beside the church. At the entrance to St Barbara's, in a chapel called **Ogrójec** (Gethsemane), is a sculptural group in limestone attributed by some to Veit Stoss, portraying *Christ on the Mount of Olives* in the act of praying surrounded by the sleeping Apostles. The group is protected behind two arches made between 1488 and 1518, enclosed by elegant gates.

Opposite and above, two views of the façade of the Church of St Barbara showing the Ogrójec portico. Below left is the 17th-century altar.

Plaques on Plac Mariacki, the former site of St. Mary's Cemetery: below centre is a sundial set into the wall of the Church of the Virgin; on the right from the top are two 16th-century plaques and one to the memory of the Jesuit Stefan Bratkowski (early 20th century) on the façade of St Barbara's Church.

MAŁY RYNEK
The Small Market Square

Two aerial views of Rynek Główny and Mały Rynek separated by the churches of the Virgin Mary and St Barbara.

Opposite, the graceful façades of the buildings on the east side of Mały Rynek.

A charming passage, near the Ogrójec, links St Mary's Square to the small Mały Rynek. This little square appears on the city maps as early as 1257 and previously served as an auxiliary market. The square, sloping towards the south, is lined on its east side with a row of *medieval buildings.* Opposite these, on the west side is the Church of St Barbara and its annexes. In summer the square becomes a large open-air café filled with colourful umbrellas; a perfect place to rest and enjoy the city's architectural heritage. On cold, wet days the smart cafes and small restaurants offer the perfect retreat. In 1661 in the Szober House at no. 6 (Kamienica Szoberowska) the first Polish periodical, the weekly "Polish Mercury", was produced on the initiative of King John Casimir II and his wife Luisa Maria Gonzaga as part of a national reform programme. It had a print run of 100-250 copies. Following Szpitalna Street, leading out of the square we reach *Plac św. Ducha* (Holy Spirit Square) where two buildings attract our attention, the austere gothic architecture of Kościół św. Krzyża (Church of the Holy Cross) contrasting with the decorative exuberance of the Juliusz Słowacki Theatre.

41

KOŚCIÓŁ ŚW. KRZYŻA
The Church of the Holy Cross

Built near the city walls in the 14th century, the Church of the Holy Cross in part suggests a fortified structure. It has a nave with no side aisles and the façade fronts a solid **square tower** surmounted by a spire covered in tiles.

The rich **interior** offers a surprising contrast to its external severity. A single column in the centre of the nave supports a network of gothic fan-vaulting. The walls are covered with fine paintings; the oldest, dated to 1420 and showing *The Agony in the Garden,* is in the chapel.

The nave and the vault are decorated with renaissance *grotesque decoration*, with plant motifs in the nave and presbytery; the leaf, flower and fruit motifs are splendid in their variety. The fresco work has been attributed to Stanisław Samostrzelnik, the first Polish painter to adopt the renaissance style. The church also has a fine bronze *baptismal font* of 1423. The late-gothic wooden *choir stalls* bear witness to the extremely high quality of inlay-work in Krakow in the 15th century.

At the end of the 19th century the Church of the Holy Cross was adopted by the actors of Krakow as their own church and its association with actors continues today on account of the neighbouring Juliusz Słowacki Theatre.

The nave and the gothic vault decorated with grotesques in the Holy Cross Church.

The bell tower of Holy Cross Church.

THE JULIUSZ SŁOWACKI THEATRE

In the 19th century Krakow was, and indeed still is today, a city in which artists were particularly favoured. It was here that Helena Modrzejewska began her career, and Konrad Swinarski and Tadeusz Kantor. During the Nazi occupation the clandestine Rhapsodic Theatre came into being with Karol Wojtyła, the future John Paul II, among its actors. The Juliusz Słowacki Theatre was built between 1890 and 1893 as the new city theatre and was considered to have one of the most technically advanced stages in the world. The first electricity plant in the city was destined for the exclusive use of the theatre. The theatre **façade** is extraordinary in the richness of its *sculptural decoration*. The various rooms which have preserved their original appearance perfectly reflect the taste of the period.

Particularly splendid is the *drop curtain* painted by the Polish artist Henryk Siemiradzki. The first production in October 1893 brought together Polish cultural figures from all over the world. Named after the great romantic poet Juliusz Słowacki (1809-49), the building was designed by the Krakowian architect Jan Zawiejski (1854-1922) who was strongly influenced by the Opéra in Paris. The theatre can house an audience of more than 920 and has exceptionally good acoustics.

The Juliusz Słowacki Theatre and the two statues on the façade from the sculptural group "Time for a Polonaise!".

BRAMA FLORIAŃSKA
St Florian's Gate

St Florian's Gate, which controlled the main access to city, is first mentioned in 1307 and was dedicated to the city's patron saint. At the beginning of the 14th century the square stone **tower** was built above the gate. Remains of the old city wall are visible on both sides. Today the tower is a favourite exhibition space for local artists. On the north side is the *white eagle*, sculpted to a design by Jan Matejko, while on the south side is a baroque bas-relief depicting *St Florian*, patron saint of the Fire Brigade, extinguishing a fire. Much venerated in Central Europe, the saint was increasingly revered in 16th-century Krakow when he was believed to have saved the Kleparz district from destruction by a dreadful fire. A Roman soldier of the 3rd century at the time of the emperor Diocletian, it is said that he extinguished a fire using a single bucket of water, the attribute with which he is often represented. The Church of St Florian was founded in 1184 by Casimir the Just to house the tomb of the saint, later removed to the Cathedral at Wawel.

Opposite page: St Florian's Gate.

Protecting the city, the statue of St Florian extinguishing a fire with a bucket of water is located over the St Florian's Gate, the main entrance in the old town walls.

THE ARTISTS OF BRAMA FLORIAŃSKA

All year round the brightly coloured open-air gallery beneath the medieval walls provides a spontaneous exhibition. Under the statue of St Florian, amateur artists offer their works for sale – an essential stopping place for lovers of this kind of art.

THE WALLS AND BATTLEMENTS

Building of Krakow's oldest ring of walls began in 1285 on the orders of prince Leszek the Black as protection against the continual attacks of the Tartars who had razed the city in 1241. In the 15th century the entire historic centre of Krakow was surrounded by a moat and a strengthened double wall which had a total of 47 square and round towers and 8 gateways, providing more than adequate defense for the city. Dismantled in the early 19th century to make way for the Planty park and gardens, only one section near to the St Florian's Gate has survived, representing in fact the earliest part of the structure. The monumental group of buildings at **Brama Floriańska** includes the **battlements**, the sections of wall with the **Ciesielska** (Joiners' Tower), the **Stolarska** (Carpenters' Tower), the **Baszta Pasamoników** (Haberdashers' Tower), the **Barbican** and 16th-century **Arsenal**. Bronze plaques along the tree-lined avenues of Planty indicate where the old ramparts stood. The *Droga Królewska* (Royal Road), began from Brama Floriańska, and on special occasions the royal procession continued from here to Ulica Floriańska, crossing Rynek Główny and Ulica Grodzka before arriving at Wawel Castle. The tourist route along the battlements of the old city walls also includes a visit to the Barbican.

Opposite page: the Haberdashers' Tower and the Carpenters' Tower on either side of Brama Floriańska.

The battlements walk in Ulica Pijarska is lively with painters and street artists around the old Arsenal. Centre, the elegant Ulica Floriańska, at the end of which the towers of Kościół Mariacki can be seen, links Brama Floriańska to Rynek Główny.

BARBAKAN
The Barbican

In the park to the north of Brama Floriańska is the Barbakan, a fortified gothic structure built to defend the main entrance to the city and now the only one of its kind in Poland still completely intact.

The Barbakan was built between 1498 and 1499 on the same spot where a defence tower once stood, the remains of which are still visible.

The rotund structure is topped with circular and octagonal pinnacles. In the sturdy walls, arranged in a chequered pattern, there are numerous openings for firearms.

The diameter of the ring of walls enclosing the Barbakan is slightly over 30 metres and the thickness of the walls varies between 300 and 365 centimetres in the lower part.

Initially, the Barbakan was linked to St Florian's Gate by a double-thick-ness wall, called *the* neck, a fragment of which can still be seen today. Its function was to pro-tect the bridge over the moat. The moat around the city centre used to be linked to that of the Barbakan while inside the fortress there were mech-anisms regulating the water level.

Two views of the massive Barbakan outside the old town walls.

MUZEUM KSIĄŻĄT CZARTORYSKICH
The Princes Czartoryski Museum

Near to St Florian's Gate the Muzeum Książąt Czartoryskich is housed in three buildings: the old Arsenal at Ulica Pijarska 8, the neighbouring Monastery and the Palace of Ulica św. Jana 19. The museum houses exhibits which are the property of either the Princes Czartoryski Foundation or the National Museum in Krakow.

This important section of the National Museum in Krakow includes a Gallery of European Painting – with some masterpieces –, a rare collection of antique European crafts and some *Memorabilia* from Puławy, a collection of arms, a section of Egyptian, Greek and Roman antiquities, documents and a library.

The museum originated from the collection which the Czartoryski family assembled from the middle of the 18th century and exhibited in Puławy from 1800, in the building known as the Temple of Sibyl, created especially to house the works, and therefore the first museum of its kind in Poland.

During the Second World War part of this treasure was lost including a *portrait study* by Raphael. In 1950 the museum became part of the National Museum in Krakow. Among the most outstanding works in the collection are the portrait of *The Lady with an Ermine* by Leonardo da Vinci and a *Landscape with the Good Samaritan* by Rembrandt van Rijn.

The building of the old Arsenal where a section of the Princes Czartoryski Museum is housed.

A statue of Mercury at the entrance of the old Arsenal.

On the second floor of the Palace, the **Gallery of European Painting** includes a Rembrandt Room as well as an important collection of Italian painting.

Rembrandt van Rjin (1609-69), **Landscape with the Good Samaritan**, 1638

The pride of the collection of 17th-century Dutch and Flemish paintings is the *Landscape with the Good Samaritan* by Rembrandt (1638) based on a story in the gospel of St Luke (X, 30-37). The painting is one of six oil paintings by the artist.

Pieter Brueghel, the Younger (1564/65-1637) **The Preaching of St. John the Baptist**, 1601-04

A copy of a painting by Brueghel the Elder, illustrating St John preaching to the crowd which had gathered in the Jordan Valley from Jerusalem. This subject was much favoured by Dutch painters in the 16th and 17th centuries as it referred to the contemporary debate on the Calvinist custom of preaching in public places.

Leonardo da Vinci (1452-1519) **The Lady with an Ermine**, c. 1490

One of Leonardo's most important female portraits is of Cecilia Galerani, a lady-in-waiting at the court and mistress of Ludovico Sforza, 'Il Moro'. The ermine which she is holding is a reference to the duke who was also known as the Ermine.

Follower of Dirk Bouts, Netherlandish School, Louvain
Christ Salvator Mundi, late 15th century
The painting is by a follower of Dirk Bouts (c. 1410-75) a Flemish
artist, famous for his portraits, who was influenced by the work
of Rogier van der Weyden.

Virgin with Child
Spain, 13th century

The Clarisse Master
Tryptych, Madonna and Child, Crucifixion, Entombment
Italy, Siena, 2nd half 13th century
The work is by Rinaldo da Siena, also known as the Clarisse Master, a painter of the Sienese School during the second half of the 13th century. Still close to the Byzantine tradition and reflecting the delicacy of Cimabue's works, the greatest master of this style was Duccio di Buoninsegna.

Master of the Pietà,
active c. 1350-80
The Crucifixion
Italian School, Siena

Michele da Verona
(c. 1470-1536/44)
Brutus and Portia
Italian School, Verona.
The painting illustrates
Portia questioning her
husband Brutus about
the secrets that are
troubling them, while in
the garden he reflects
anxiously on the plot
he is organising against
Julius Caesar.

Lorenzo Lotto
(1480-1556), **Adoration of
the Child**, c. 1508
Frequently represented by
Lorenzo Lotto, the subject
of the "Adoration of the
Child" is one of the oldest
subjects in Christian art.

*Works of the most important
ancient civilizations are
exhibited in the large room
housing the **Gallery of
Antiquities** on the first floor of
the old Arsenal. The collection
includes works from 3000 B.C. to
the 7th century A.D. The exhibits
are of various kinds: fragments
of frescoes, terracotta artefacts,
jewellery and statues in wood
and bronze. The Egyptian
collection is the pride of the
Gallery and contains important
antiquities, including two
sarcophagi carved with the
human form dating from the
9th century B.C.*

Gallery of Antiquities.

Isis with Horus
Basalt
Egyptian art, 1st century B.C.

Statuette of a naked woman
Wood
Egyptian Art, Middle Kingdom, 2000-1700 B.C. Property of the
Institute of Archaeology, Jagiellonian University in Krakow

**Etruscan sarcophagus with a lid in shape of a woman
wearing a tunic**
Terracotta
Tuscania, end of 3rd – beginning of 2nd century B.C.

The
collection
of **14th-17th
Century Polish
Antiques and European
Artistic Crafts** is housed on the
first floor of the Palace in Ulica św. Jana.

**Majolica
plate**
Italy, Deruta,
c. 1550
Majolica plate with the
Death of Zerbino from Ariosto's
Orlando Furioso. This beautiful plate is the
most important item in the museum's extensive
collection of Italian majolica.

17th-century cabinet
17th-century cabinet with biblical and genre scenes ornamented with relief intarsia.

Statuettes of Polish aristocrats.
Germany, Meissen, around 1735-1745.
A group of fine Meissen porcelain figures made by one of the most famous ceramic workers of the period.

Above, a view of the Jagiellon Room.

Housed in the **Tent Room** (in the Palace, first floor) are items and military artefacts relating to the liberation of Vienna from the Turkish siege by the Polish King John III Sobieski in 1683. These include a Turkish tent and a beautiful Turkish carpet. Many of the items were part of the spoils of war.

The Tent Room, **Hussars armour.**

The Tent Room. In foreground, **Scale armour of Mikołaj Hieronim Sieniawski**, Poland, c. 1680.

The Parade Shield
Milano, Italy, 16th century
Iliad episode: fight between Menelaus and Hector.

left all her jewels for its modernisation. The University's greatest patron then became King Władysław Jagiełło, whose Lithuanian name has been given to it ever since. The University holds a special place in Polish history, as its activity has remained uninterrupted since its foundation despite various attempts at persecution and periods of clandestine operations; in this it can be compared to the unbroken tradition of the Catholic Church in Poland.

The building takes the shape of a quadrilateral with a large **inner courtyard** and a cloistered walk with gothic arches, similar to the Wawel Castle. The Collegium Maius is enhanced by architectural features such as the decorative surrounds of the doorways and the *stone* commemorating the construction of the "Jerusalem" hostel.

The building of the Collegium Maius and below right, the internal courtyard.

Below left, votive plaque of the "Jerusalem" hostel.

Opposite page, the Jagiellonian Hall of the Collegium Maius with stalls for the professors.

COLLEGIUM MAIUS

Following Ulica Jagiellońska we reach a building which has been part of the University since the Middle Ages and is one of the oldest University buildings in the world. The Collegium Maius, dating from 1400, is now the **Historic Museum of the Jagiellonian University**. After Prague, this was the most important university in Central Europe. The Jagiellonian University grew out of the Krakow Academy, founded in 1364 by King Casimir the Great. The Academy's patron was Queen Jadwiga, daughter of Louis of Hungary, who

Opposite page, the Stuba
Communis: *some of the fine
woodwork, and the small alcove
which juts from the façade, with
the statue of Casimir the Great.*

The Libraria
of the Collegium Maius.

63

On the ground floor can be visit the rooms where lectures and courses were held. On the first floor are the reception rooms of the Krakow Athenaeum: *Libraria*, *Stuba Communis* and the *Jagiellonian Hall*. The Stuba Communis was where the University masters ate their meals until the end of the 18th century. The Jagiellonian Hall, with its coffered ceiling and stalls for the masters, provides fascinating documentation of the University's history, decorated with portraits of benefactors and patrons of the Athenaeum. The renaissance doorway bears the motto: *Plus ratio quam vis* (Reason is greater than strength).

The Historic Museum of the Jagiellonian University preserves documents and items relating to the history of the University. The most precious pieces in the collection are the alchemical and astronomical instruments and in particular a globe dated 1510, known as the **Golden Globe**, the first to indicate America (*America terra noviter reperta*).

Two of the most illustrious students to attend the University were in 1491, **Nicholas Copernicus** (1473-1543) and in the last century, **Karol Wojtyła**, the future pope John Paul II.

Collegium Maius, 15th and 16th-century astronomical intruments.

COLLEGIUM NOVUM

In the second half of the 19th century the University of Krakow made some notable advances in the field of science, including the liquefaction of oxygen in 1883 by Karol Olszewski and Zygmunt Wróblewski. On the site of the "Jerusalem" hostel, demolished in the cause of modernisation, the Collegium Novum was built to a design by Feliks Księżarski. The building contains the Rector's rooms and the principle offices of the Athenaeum. A **statue of Copernicus** stands on the lawn just outside the building.

The neo-gothic façade of the Collegium Novum.

KOŚCIÓŁ ŚW. ANNY
The Church of St Anne

The street now named Ulica św. Anny was originally known as Ulica Żydowska (Jewish Street) indicating the area where the first Jewish community of Krakow lived. The foundations of St Anne's Church located here date from the 14th century. The present church is built on an earlier gothic structure and is considered to be one of the finest examples of baroque religious architecture in Poland. Since its earliest days it has been an integral part of the University area and the most important ceremonies relating to University life, such as the official opening of the academic year, are held here. The architect Tylman van Gameren was responsible for its baroque design (1689-1703). The decoration of the **interior** represents the Church Triumphant and was mainly the work of the architect and sculptor Baldassarre Fontana who designed the spectacular and intricate *stuccowork* and sumptuous *high altar* in the style of the baroque churches of Rome created during the Counter-Reformation.

*The baroque interior of the Church of St Anne:
right, the pulpit; below left, the elaborate high altar by Baldassarre Fontana and below right, the tomb of St John Cantius.*

KOŚCIÓŁ DOMINIKANÓW
The Dominican Church

Near Ulica Grodzka are the Dominican Church and M[...]tery, the oldest buildings in Krakow to be made of bric[...] also the first examples of the gothic style in the city. Built [...] 1223, the monastery preserves remains of an earlier ston[...] manesque construction. In the presbytery there is a toml[...] to Filip Kallimach (Filippo Buonaccorsi) – tutor to the chi[...] of Casimir Jagiellon. In the north aisle a stairway leads t[...] chapel of St Hyacinth built after 1545.

The Myszkowski chapel of 1614 opens off the south aisle a[...] one of the "Sarmatian" chapels of the golden age, the first [...] the chapel of King Sigismund and the last the Vasa chapel i[...] Cathedral.

The frescoed dome of the church of St Anne and a statue in the magnificent baroque interior.

The neo-gothic timpanum over the gothic entrance to the Dominican church.

The Polish artists who worked on the church interior were also influenced by the style as can be seen in the elaborate wooden *pulpit* supported by the magnificent figure of an angel, made by Antoni Frączkiewicz, a Krakowian artist. In the right transept is the *tomb of St John Cantius* (1390-1473), a professor at the University of Krakow to whom the church was dedicated in 1689. The carefully structured composition of this sophisticated masterpiece is crowned by a 'heavenly glory' while the sarcophagus beneath is supported by four figures representing Theology, Philosophy, Law and Medicine. The bust of the saint is by Franciszek Wyspiański.

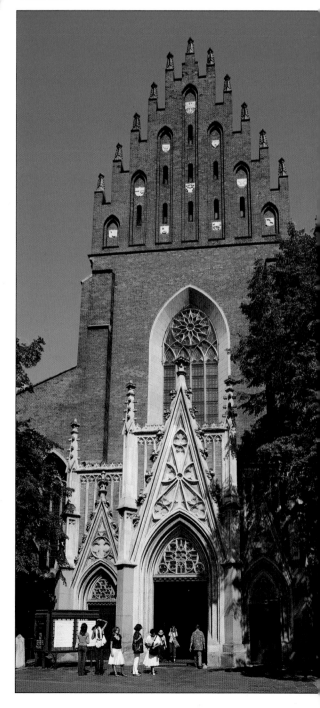

Planty

PLANTY

In keeping with many other projects to modernize older European cities, Planty was created in the 19th century to replace the old medieval city walls. This delightful park circles the Stare Miasto and its avenues provide many pleasant walks. The grounds and paths are enhanced by fountains, open spaces, monuments to famous personalities of Polish history and panoramic viewpoints. The Kościuszko Mound can be seen from the scenic point in the University area. Some of the statues depict characters from dramas by Juliusz Słowacki.

WAWEL

The Wawel hill has been described by many as the Polish Acropolis, similar to the Campidoglio in Rome or the Kremlin in Moscow. Over the centuries the area has confirmed its role as the nation's sanctuary, representing the religious and patriotic ideals of Poland, and symbolising the continuity of national religious and political traditions.

Standing on the hill are both the Castle, representing the ancient splendour of the kings, and the Cathedral, point of reference for Krakow's large diocese, pantheon of the country's sovereigns and Polish heroes, centre of the cults of St Stanisław and St Jadwiga.

Since 1320 the Wawel cathedral has been the location for the coronation and burial of kings: buried in the crypts are the last Jagiellons, Sigismund the Old and Sigismund II the August, the Vasa kings, Sigismund III, Władysław IV and John II Casimir and their wives and children. In the ancient crypt of St Leonard, dating from the 11th century, Tadeusz Kościuszko is buried and Karol Wojtyła celebrated his first mass on 2 November 1946.

The various structures that have been built on this hill have mingled and overlapped to create a combination of **architectural styles** that is of incomparable historic and artistic value. Several important periods can be identified in the history of Wawel. In the earliest times, around 1000 A.D., the seat of the bishopric of Krakow was here. Remains can still be seen of the ancient Church of the Virgin Mary, slightly to the north of which the first stone Cathedral was built; the romanesque crypt of St Leonard was created in the vaults. Under Leszek the Black and his successors in the 13th century a castle was built on Wawel in the early gothic style, with stone ramparts for protection

against continual attacks by the Mongols. During the 14th century the Castle was protected by a ring of walls and towers, and royal apartments and accommodation for the court were added. At the same time the Cathedral was rebuilt in gothic style. Around the 1350s Casimir the Great restructured and extended the Castle, also in gothic style, introducing a splendour previously unknown to the area. The Jagiellon kings added magnificent renaissance structures to the Castle in the 16th century, inspired by elegant Italian palaces of the day. During this period the sumptuous

Sigismund chapel, designed by the Florentine Bartolomeo Berrecci, was added to the Cathedral. Following a fire in 1595, the Vasa dynasty renovated the buildings in baroque style. In recent times Wawel has developed its historic characteristics becoming an area of museums and an important destination for tourists. The entire complex has been carefully restored and its artistic heritage is now coordinated by the **Zamek Królewski na Wawelu - Panstwowe Zbiory Sztuki** (National Collection of the Arts of Poland – Royal Castle of Wawel).

Aerial view of Wawel looking towards the Old Town. In the foreground is the Thieves' Tower and the Sandomierz Tower. On the left is the Cathedral and on the right the buildings of the Royal Castle.

The oldest views of Krakow show a city clustered at the bottom of a hill and protected by fortifications. The *Wawel hill* has always dominated the city's panorama. Rising some 28 metres above the city, the south side of the hill directly overlooks the *Vistula* towards which a rock face of Jurassic limestone once dropped. From as early as Palaeolithic times men lived in the caves carved into the rock by the river water. The first stable settlements on the Wawel hill appeared some 5000 years ago and were followed by Neolithic peasant communities, Bronze Age, and then later Iron Age, settlers. Archaeological excavations have revealed that in the 6th century a fortified settlement existed at the top of the hill and there are traces of a Christian church dating from the 9th century. For centuries a small fortified town stood at the summit with the castle of the ruler, later the king, at its centre.

THE BUILDINGS OF WAWEL

For centuries the skyline of Wawel has been dominated by the ring of **ramparts**, the bulk of the **Royal Castle** (Zamek) with its **towers**, and the **Cathedral** (Katedra) buildings with the three **towers**, the **chapels** and **crypts**.

A visit to the **Dragon's Den (**Smocza Jama) begins at the foot of the Thieves' Tower. This cavern, some 270 metres long, 81 of which can be visited, represents one of the myths surrounding the origins of Krakow. The priests of the Cathedral live in the **Vicar's House** (Wikarówka). The buildings to the north-west are occupied by the offices and staff of the Wawel Museums.

The old royal kitchens now house the permanent exhibition **"Lost Wawel"** (Wawel zaginiony) where remains of the old fortifications, remnants from the romanesque period such as the lovely *Rotunda* from the apse of the Church of the Virgin Mary, and plans of the Castle from the 11th century up to the gothic period are displayed. The **Halls** and the **Royal Apartments** are most impressive and house collections of art, the **Crown Treasury and Armoury** (Skarbiec Koronny i Zbrojownia) and the collection of **Oriental Art** (Sztuka Wschodu).

An **archaeological site** in front of the Royal Castle has revealed the foundations of medieval religious buildings. The **Cathedral Museum** is housed in one of the chapter houses beside the Vasa Gate and was opened in 1978 by Karol Wojtyła, at the time cardinal of Krakow.

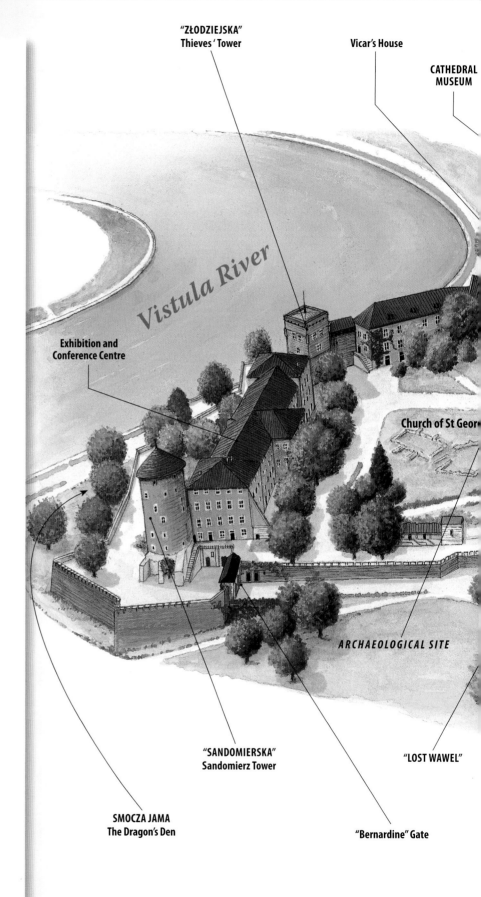

"ZŁODZIEJSKA"
Thieves' Tower

Vicar's House

CATHEDRAL MUSEUM

Vistula River

Exhibition and Conference Centre

Church of St George

ARCHAEOLOGICAL SITE

"SANDOMIERSKA"
Sandomierz Tower

"LOST WAWEL"

SMOCZA JAMA
The Dragon's Den

"Bernardine" Gate

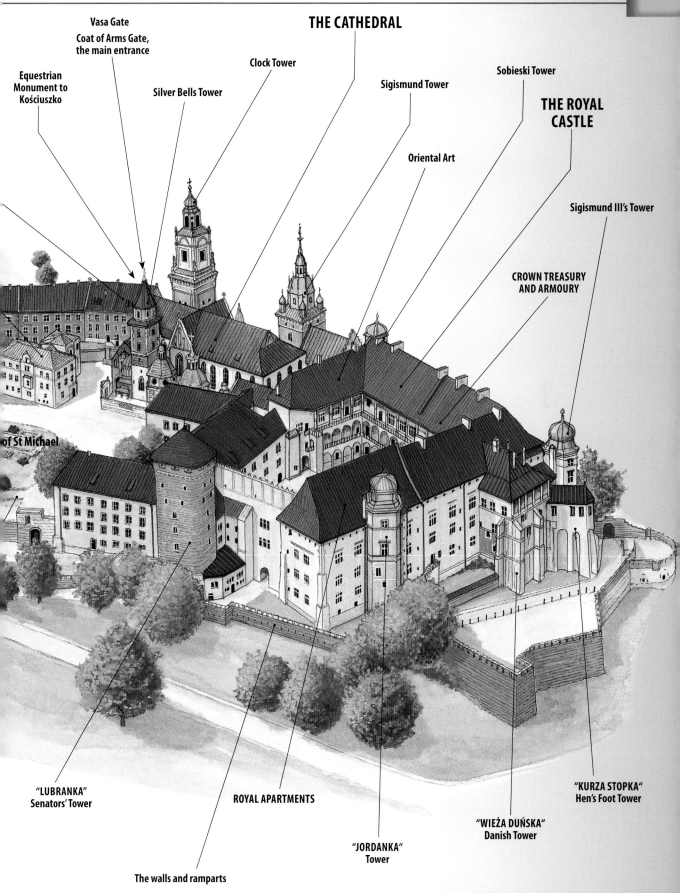

Equestrian
Monument to
Kościuszko

Vasa Gate

Coat of Arms Gate,
the main entrance

Silver Bells Tower

Clock Tower

THE CATHEDRAL

Sigismund Tower

Oriental Art

Sobieski Tower

**THE ROYAL
CASTLE**

Sigismund III's Tower

**CROWN TREASURY
AND ARMOURY**

of St Michael

"LUBRANKA"
Senators' Tower

ROYAL APARTMENTS

The walls and ramparts

"JORDANKA"
Tower

"WIEŻA DUŃSKA"
Danish Tower

"KURZA STOPKA"
Hen's Foot Tower

THE TOWERS OF WAWEL

The defensive system of the towers of Wawel developed during the 11th century when the Cathedral was fortified with four towers of which the only remaining original part is the lower section of Silver Bells Tower.

In the 14th century the romanesque buildings were rebuilt in gothic style and a new ring of walls was built with a series of towers: three of these towers are the **"Złodziejska"** (Thieves' Tower) on the side overlooking the Vistula, the **"Kurza Stopka"** (Hen's Foot Tower) in the gothic area of the Royal Palace, and beside it the slightly later square tower, **Wieża Duńska** (Danish Tower).

The most impressive towers of Wawel were built in the second half of the 15th century by the Jagiellons – the **"Lubranka"** (Senators' Tower), beside the palace and the **"Sandomierska"** (Sandomierz Tower), on the southern ramparts. This last tower is named after the nobles from the region of Sandomierz who were imprisoned there.

From top: the Sandomierz Tower surmounting the "Bernardine" Gate; looking towards the Stradom district the Thieves' Tower and the Senators' Tower can be seen.

THE ROAD TO WAWEL

The road leading from the Old Town to Wawel was for many centuries the only link between the low-land and the top of the hill. The old road leads along the north wing of the Castle and ascends parallel to the left side of the Cathedral with its two towers, the Sigismund Tower and the Clock Tower.

The road is flanked by a wall covered in **plaques**. These commemorate all those who helped to restore Wawel after the years of damage suffered under the Austrian occupation.

SMOCZA JAMA

The Dragon's Den

The legend of the Wawel dragon relates the mythical origins of Krakow and is part of the Polish **Chronicles** (*Kronika Polonorum*) compiled by Vincent Kadłubek in the 12th century. The story goes that a terrible dragon ate cows and men, frightening the inhabitants of Krakow. One day Prince Grakch, whom the locals came to call Krak (and hence the city's name), arrived from Carinthia and on being proclaimed king decided to kill the monstrous dragon. Grakch's sons threw a cow stuffed with sulphur into the cave whereupon the beast ate it and died.

Above, the wall of the Road to Wawel leading to the north entrance.

Left and below right, two views of Dragon's Den, the legendary cave in the western slope of Wawel hill.

Below left, the metal sculpture of the Wawel Dragon (1970) by Bronisław Chromy placed in front of the Dragon's Den.

KATEDRA
The Cathedral

The first cathedral was built on Wawel about 1020 when Emperor Otto III gave his consent to King Bolesław I the Brave to institute the Polish ecclesiastical hierarchy. All that remains of the first cathedral is the crypt dedicated to St Gereon, while surviving elements of the second, romanesque building are the St Leonard crypt, the lower part of the **Wieża Srebrnych Dzwonów** (Silver Bells Tower), and the base of the **Wieża Zegarowa** (Clock Tower) which is gothic with baroque crowning. The **Wieża Zygmuntowska** (Sigismund Tower) takes its name from King Sigismund the Elder, as does its enormous **bell** (the entrance to the tower is in the Cathedral sacristy).

The bell was cast in 1520 and exemplifies Polish bell-founding at its greatest. The gothic cathedral we see today is therefore the third ecclesiastical building. Work began on the present construction in 1320 and it was consecrated in 1364. Over the centuries the Cathedral has been enlarged, new chapels have been added and the building has been made higher.

During the mid 13th century the Cathedral became the centre of the cult of St Stanisław.

The **south side** of the Cathedral is interesting for the variety of architectural styles and elements it incorporates, from the romanesque to modern additions. Two chapels flanking the main gothic structure are remarkable for their similarity: the renaissance **Kaplica Zygmuntowska** (King Sigismund chapel), covered with a gilt dome, and the baroque **Kaplica Wazów** (Vasa chapel), a hundred years later than the first but with an identical ground plan. The spherical vault of the Kaplica Zygmuntowska is coated with gold leaf of enormous value which no invader has ever dared to vandalise.

Opposite page, part of the south side of the Cathedral with the dome of the Vasa chapel in the centre and the gilded dome of King Sigismund chapel.

The statue of St Sigismund, one of the four statues around the dome of the Vasa chapel.

From the left, the Sigismund Tower, the Clock Tower and the Silver Bells Tower, rising in the background.

PLAN OF THE CATHEDRAL

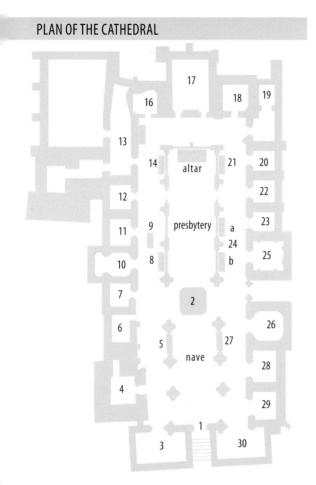

1- Door decorated in iron, bearing the initials of Casimir the Great
2- Mausoleum of St Stanisław
3- Chapel of the Holy Trinity
4- Czartoryski Chapel, entrance to the crypt with the tombs of the kings
5- Funerary monument to Władysław Warneńczyk
6- St Nicholas Chapel
7- Bishop Maciejowski Chapel
8- Silver plaque depicting John III Sobieski before Vienna
9- Mickiewicz and Słowacki crypt
10- Lipski Chapel
11- Skotnicki Chapel
12- Bishop Zebrzydowski Chapel
13- Sacristy - corridor leading to the Sigismund Tower
14- Funerary monument to Władysław the Short
15- Altar to the Crucified Christ (the black gothic Crucifix)
16- Bishop Gamrat Chapel
17- Lady Chapel with the funerary monument to Stefan Batory
18- Bishop Tomicki Chapel
19- Bishop Załuski Chapel
20- John Albert Chapel
21- Funerary monument to Casimir the Great
22- Bishop Zadzik Chapel
23- Bishop Konarski Chapel
24 *a b*- Royal insignia of Queen Jadwiga and her funerary monument
25- Sigismund Chapel
26- Vasa Chapel
27- Funerary monument to Władysław Jagiełło
28- Szafraniec Chapel
29- Potocki Chapel
30- Holy Cross Chapel

THE INTERIOR

The black stone portal with wooden doors covered in metal bearing one of the symbols of Krakow, the initial K of King Casimir the Great surmounted by a crown, leads into the Cathedral. In the great nave we are immediately confronted with the **St Stanisław Mausoleum**, a monument of enormous religious significance and of considerable artistic interest.

The *silver sarcophagus* containing the remains of the saint is a masterpiece of 17th-century goldsmiths' work. It was made in 1670 in Gdańsk in the workshop of Peter van der Rennen, and is decorated with twelve reliefs depicting scenes from the Saint's life together with the miracles attributed to him after his death. The black marble *baldachin* above the sarcophagus is an earlier work by Giovanni Trevano (1626-30).

Opposite page, two views of the Cathedral with the Mausoleum of St Stanisław.

Above, the gothic central nave with the Mausoleum of St Stanisław containing the saint's tabernacle. On the right is the tomb of King Ladislaus (Władysław) Jagiełło and one of the antique tapestries that enhance the Cathedral.

A detail of the Cathedral's splendid stained glass windows.

THE TOMBS OF THE KINGS

The sculptural effigies on the tombs of the Polish kings and bishops are the most important group of monuments inside the Cathedral. They were carved by famous Polish sculptors and foreign artists working in Poland, including Veit Stoss, Bartolomeo Berrecci, Jan Michałowicz of Urzędów, Santi Gucci and Antoni Madeyski. Madeyski (1869-1939) was responsible for two of the funerary monuments: those of Władysław III and of Queen Jadwiga. The tomb of King Władysław is empty. The body of the young king, killed in the battle of Varna (1444) while leading a daring attack against the Janissaries, was never recovered. The remains of **Queen Jadwiga** were placed in her tomb in 1949. The daughter of Louis d'Anjou, King of Hungary, and great-granddaughter of Władysław the Short, she succeeded to the Polish throne at the age

The baroque interior of the dome in the Vasa chapel.

St Stanisław of Szczepanowo was bishop of Krakow from 1072 until his death in 1079, and the legend of his life and death is related in the *Chronicles* of Vincent Kadłubek, although the events he recalls in 1200 are not fully confirmed by other historical evidence. What is certain is that the dramatic conflict between Bishop Stanisław and King Bolesław II the Bold was of a political nature and ended in the bishop's death by quartering. The spread of the cult of the Bishop-Martyr led to his canonisation in 1253 and from that time his tomb has been a centre of pilgrimage.

of ten. She was renowned for her saintliness during her lifetime, and after her death at the end of the 15th century her cult spread. In 1949 her tomb was opened and her remains were moved to the sepulchre of white Carrara marble carved by Madeyski. This work with its cold harmony and classical linearity is decorated with a frieze of eagles around the sides and reflects a fully modernist style. Between 1387 and 1390 the Chapel to the Virgin was built, originally fulfilling the role of a minor choir. At the end of the 16th century Anna Jagiellonka had the chapel transformed into the **funerary chapel for Stefan I Batory** and the marble monument to the king by the Florentine Santi Gucci was placed there. Gucci, a master of the mannerist style, worked in Krakow for many years. The figure of the king, sculpted in low-relief, does not appear to be a likeness in death but rather the portrait of a sleeping man with a soft smile on his lips and making a natural gesture with his hand. The details in black marble were added in 1648 by the Vasa who showed particular enthusiasm for this material.

Chapel of the Holy Cross with the tomb of Bishop Kajetan Sołtyk.

The funerary chapel of King Stefan Batory with the image of the Black Madonna of Częstochowa. On the left wall is the royal sepulchre designed by Santi Gucci in the 16th century.

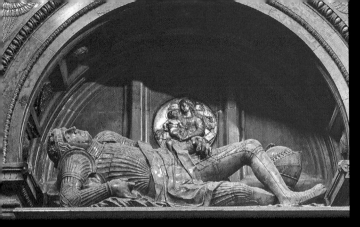

KAPLICA ZYGMUNTOWSKA
The King Sigismund chapel

Kaplica Zygmuntowska differs from all the other chapels in the Cathedral for the purity of its style, never having undergone restoration. It was built by Bartolomeo Berrecci from Pontassieve near Florence, who was summoned to Krakow by Sigismund I. The first drawings for the chapel were presented to the king in 1517, and in 1519 the foundations were laid.

Three colour tones dominate the interior: the gold of the inscriptions, the brilliant white of the walls and the unusual red marble of the monuments to *Sigismund I* and his children *Sigismund Augustus* and *Anna Jagiellonka*. The square plan covered by a dome is in pure renaissance style. The funerary slab to Anna Jagiellonka, placed there in 1596, was carved while the queen was still alive.

Chapel of King Sigismund: the tombs of the last Jagiellons (top) and a detail of the tomb of Queen Anna Jagiellonka

Presbytery: the tomb of the blessed Queen Jadwiga Jagiellon, in white Carrara marble by Antoni Madeyski.

Above, the building which houses the Cathedral Museum,
beside the Vasa Gate. Right, the entrance to the Cathedral, on the east
side of the Cathedral Museum.

MUZEUM KATEDRALNE
JANA PAWŁA II
The John Paul II Cathedral Museum

The Cathedral Museum and Treasury was established in 1906 by cardinal Jan Puzyna and is one of the most important collections of sacred art assembled in the 20th century. In addition to the objects belonging to the Cathedral Treasury, the museum also houses bequests from many other churches of the Archdiocese of Krakow including a collection of 14th-century paintings. Sculptures, vases, reliquaries, decorations, liturgical items and 16th-century Flemish tapestries are all displayed, the insignia and instruments of Polish royalty are also exhibited, such as the sceptre of wood and the pommel of Queen Jadwiga (1374-99) who is buried in the Cathedral. Many embroidered fabrics are also on display, including the ***ornat Kmity*** (the Kmita chasuble), a fine masterpiece of late 15th-century embroidery presented by the governor of the province of Krakow, Piotr Kmita in 1503, on the 250th anniversary of the canonization of Saint Stanisław. The precious embroidered chasuble is dedicated to the martyr saint and represents lifelike scenes in relief, similar to the best Polish gothic sculpture.

Beside it stands the gothic pavilion with a large terrace: this was added during the reign of Jadwiga of Anjou and Władysław Jagiełło in the late 14th century. The most notable changes were made when, after the disastrous fire of 1499, King Alexander and his brother Sigismund undertook the reconstruction of the Castle in renaissance style. Following a second fire some of the rooms were enriched with baroque decoration. During the 19th century the Austrian occupation caused considerable damage to the Castle. The dedication of groups of citizens led to the reconstruction of the Wawel buildings in 1905, and under Franz Josef restoration of the monumental interiors was begun.

Part of the ramparts in the walls on the side towards Stare Miasto.

ZAMEK
The Royal Castle

Archaeological excavations have confirmed that the first royal court was housed in a stone building constructed between the 10th and 11th centuries. At the beginning of the 12th century a romanesque fortified castle stood on the hill, while the first gothic structure was built by Władysław the Short who sought to strengthen Krakow's role as a capital city. His son Casimir the Great (1333-70), responsible for the construction of a large number of castles in Poland in the 14th century, built an impressive gothic castle on the hill of which only the *Kurza Stopka* (Hens's foot) Tower remains.

THE GOTHIC WING

Top, the fortified buildings of the medieval wing in the north-east corner of the castle, consisting of the small watch-tower known as the *Kurza Stopka* (Hen's Foot) Tower, overlooking the Old Town and, on the left, the Danish Tower, both dated 14th century. Of a later date, *Sigismund III's Tower*, is seen in the background.

THE COURTYARD
OF THE ROYAL CASTLE

The Castle courtyard is one of the finest examples of Italian renaissance architecture in Poland. Built in such a grand style, the Royal Castle on Wawel was intended to reflect the magnificence of Sigismund the Elder and the extent of the power of the Jagiellonian dynasty, which at the beginning of the 16th century extended over Poland, Lithuania, Bohemia and Hungary, covering an area from the Baltic to the Adriatic, from the source of the Elbe to the Dneiper.

The portico and the first two orders of arcading surrounding the courtyard form covered walks which on the ground and first floors are protected by renaissance arches, while on the top storey protection from the damp climate is provided by a steeply sloping roof with gutters, supported by slender columns. Fragments of 16th-century frescoes are still visible on the walls.

Along the south side there is a wall, also decorated with arches and with trompe l'œil windows in which we see the sky and the tops of the trees growing on the Ulica Bernardyńska side of the hill.

The large renaissance court of the castle, the loggia on the second floor and, below, details of the original wall frescoes.

THE ROYAL APARTMENTS

Traditionally in Central Europe the ground floor was reserved for the servants and administrative functions, on the first floor were the royal apartments and chambers for members of the court and guests, while the reception rooms were located on the second floor. Of particular interest on the first floor are the renaissance and gothic doorways, the 16th century furnishings with North European and Italian items, the original gothic rooms of the **Hen's Foot Tower** and the neo-classical **Column Hall**.

On the second floor other rooms of interest are the **Bird Room**, the 17th-century **Royal Chapel** and the **Hall of Deputies** where the elaborate ceiling is decorated with carved and painted wooden heads.

The beautiful antique leather wall coverings date from the 18th century and are known as the *Cordovans*.

On the second floor:

the Bird Room where the walls are covered with 18th-century Cordovans and, below, the 17th-century Royal Chapel showing the fine stucco-work in the vault.

Opposite page, two views of the Senators' Room showing the collection of tapestries which belonged to Sigismund II Augustus, illustrating the Story of Noah (below and following page).

The neo-classical Column Hall, or the Merlini Room, on the first floor.

A 15th-century tondo of the Florentine School, in the Wawel gallery.

THE WAWEL COLLECTIONS

The rich collection of **tapestries** decorating the castle walls are the finest examples of renaissance art in Poland. The survival of these remarkable works provides the museum interiors with an impressive reminder of the Castle's original splendour. The collection, which consisted of 365 tapestries at the end of the 16th century, grew from a series of sixteen made in the Gobelin style and commissioned by Sigismund I from the Antwerp workshop in 1526. The **picture gallery** includes works by Polish artists and other European schools, either donated to or purchased by the museum. These include the portraits of sovereigns and Polish magnates painted by Krakowian artists and commissioned by the court, baroque paintings, mostly Flemish and Dutch, as well as Italian works of the 15th and 16th centuries. One of these is the 15th-century tondo of the Florentine school showing the *Christ Child, the Madonna, St Joseph and the Angel Gabriel.*

OKÓŁ
STRADOM

Probably the oldest city suburb, Okół began to develop on the lower reaches of Wawel about 1000, extending around a large market area, later to be named Mary Magdalene Square. To the south-east is the historic district of Stradom where in the past the road for transporting salt from the Wieliczka mines ran.

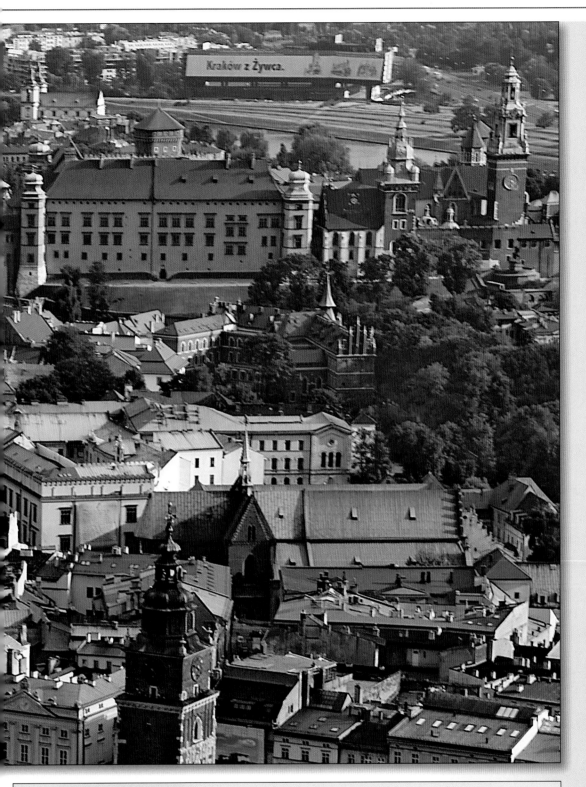

House Under the Lion

Dom Pod Lwem, Ulica Grodzka, 32.

In bygone times the houses of Krakow were not numbered and they were therefore named for the sign above the doorway: House of Angels, the Elephant House, and so on. The bas-relief of the Lion seen here is of the gothic period.

Pałac Biskupa Erazma Ciołka, The Bishop Erasmus Ciołek Palace, Ulica Kanonicza 17

The National Museum in Krakow. Art of Old Poland.

The 12th-18th-Century Orthodox Art of the Old Polish Republic

The residence of Bishop Erasmus Ciołek was refurbished to house the section of the National Museum in Krakow where Polish art from the Middle Ages to the baroque period is displayed. Restoration brought to light the early Renaissance splendours of the building.

The highlight of the museum is the *Virgin with Child from Krużlowa*. This polychrome statue, 118 cm high, was transferred from the parish church in Krużlowa to the National Museum in 1899. It is representative of works known as the "**Beautiful Madonnas**" which first appeared in French stone statuary and later in wooden sculpture in Central Europe. The characteristic feature of all these pieces is the curve of the Madonna's body into an "S" shape. The treatment of the drapery and the Mother's tender idealised expression suggest that the Krużlowa Madonna was carved circa 1420.

*Leaving Wawel in the direction of Rynek Główny we reach Okół where we can choose to follow either Ulica Grodzka, the old Droga Królewska (Royal Route) or picturesque route along the **Ulica Kanonicza**, flanked by elegant historic buildings; some of these now house important institutions such as the **Archdiocesan Museum** at no. 19-21, the **John Paul II Institute** at no. 18, and the **Cricoteka** at no. 5, the Centre for the Documentation of the Art of Tadeusz Kantor and his famous Cricot 2 theatre.*

ARCHDIOCESAN MUSEUM

Located at **numbers 19-21 of Ulica Kanonicza**, where Karol Wojtyła lived when he was bishop and archbishop of Krakow, is the Archdiocesan Museum which opened in 1994 to house the precious collection of religious art and artifacts assembled over time by the Archdiocese of Krakow. The valuable sacred items displayed here include works from Kościół Mariacki and the churches of Dębno and Korzkiew. The Museum is divided into sections for **paintings**, **sculptures** and **applied arts**, and exhibitions are often held here to promote modern religious art.

The building which houses the Archdiocesan Museum with the towers of Wawel in the background.

*The John Paul II Institute:
below, a coin with a portrait of pope
John Paul II and above, documents including a
diploma in Theology from Krakow University.*

*On the right from above, a reconstruction of
Wojtyła's room as it was in the Dean's House,
and one of the exhibition rooms.*

THE JOHN PAUL II INSTITUTE

Founded in 1995, the Institute was visited and blessed by Pope John Paul II on 9 June 1997, during his pilgrimage to Poland. The mission of the Institute is to promote the memory of Karol Wojtyła and his work, continuing and spreading his religious teaching and writings starting from his early days as a priest at St Florian's Church in Krakow in 1949-50. The Institute has a *library* providing fundamental documentation for studying the life and works of John Paul, and organizes seminars, lectures and conferences.

The building in which it is housed is a beautiful 14th-century structure at no. **18 Kanonicza Street**, a historic property belonging to the church of Krakow.

DOM DZIEKAŃSKI
The Dean's House

This beautiful house at **no. 21 of Ulica Kanonicza** is one of the most beautiful properties belonging to the church in Krakow. Of medieval origin, it was furnished by the Italian sculptor and architect, Santi Gucci. The courtyard and façade decorated with friezes date from this period. Above the majestic doorway in classical style is Virgil's admonition "Procul este, profani" (Hence, far hence, ye uninitiated).

Karol Wojtyła lived here in the years 1958-67. Previously, from 1951, he had lived in the neighbouring house, no. 19. At present, the Museum of the Krakow Archdiocese is housed in both buildings.

KOŚCIÓŁ ŚW. BERNARDYNA
The Church of St Bernardin

In *Stradom*, at the foot of Wawel, in Bernardyńska Street, stands the church dedicated to St Bernardin of Siena. The baroque church was built between 1670 and 1680 to replace the gothic structure of some 200 years earlier and destroyed by the Swedes in 1655. The sumptuous baroque **interior** is still intact. The painting of the Virgin of Sokal, crowned in 1724, is in the Sanctuary of the Virgin. In the north chapel there is a sculpture of *St Anne with the Virgin and Child* attributed to Veit Stoss.

KOŚCIÓŁ ŚW. ANDRZEJA
The Church of St Andrew

Built with blocks of white limestone, Kościół św. Andrzeja is the best preserved romanesque church in Krakow and was fortified in the 13th century for protection against attack by the Tartars. The façade looking on to Ulica Grodzka is flanked by two towers with square bases which become octagonal at the height of the roof of the nave. The lanterns on top of the towers were built in 1639. The baroque interior has a small treasury with one of the oldest cribs in Europe.

Opposite, a view of Dom Dziekański.

The interior of the Church of St Bernardin rebuilt and decorated in the baroque style.

The romanesque Church of St Andrew on Ulica Grodzka.

Ulica Grodzka *is the main tourist route connecting Market Square with Wawel. Many buildings of great historic interest are situated along this road, including the* ***Collegium Juridicum*** *at no. 43, owned by the University since 1403. The important collection of the* ***Muzeum Archeologiczne*** *(Archaeological Museum) is housed nearby in Ulica Senacka. On the east side of Ulica Grodzka are two churches built in contrasting styles – the baroque* ***Church of St Peter and St Paul*** *and the romanesque* ***Church of St Andrew***.

KOŚCIÓŁ
ŚW. ŚW. PIOTRA I PAWŁA
The Church of Sts Peter and Paul

The Church of Sts Peter and Paul, designed by Giovanni De Rosis, is the oldest baroque church in Krakow and was strongly influenced by Italian baroque architecture, especially by the churches of the Gesù and of Sant'Andrea della Valle in Rome. It was built after the arrival of the Jesuits in Poland in 1583. On the far left side of the façade is the statue of Ignatius of Loyola, spiritual father of the Jesuits and the founder of the Society of Jesus. **Inside**, above the crossing is a large dome decorated by Giovan Battista Falconi, the first baroque sculptor to work in Krakow. He was also responsible for the stucco decoration in the **apse** depicting the *Death of St Peter and St Paul*. The dome was completed in 1619 and its decoration in 1633.

THE TWELVE APOSTLES

The small square in front of the Church of Sts Peter and Paul is enclosed by ele wrought-iron railings including twelve tall pedestals supporting baroque stat white stone of the twelve Apostles. They are the work of Daniel (or perhaps of Hell and of Ferdinand Kilcz. The soft stone from which they are sculpted has su considerably over the years from erosion and the statues now in the square ar of the originals made by Kazimierz Jęczmyk and Ryszard Ochęduszko.

Statues of the twelve Apostles on the railings in front of the Church of Sts Peter and Paul.

Above, the façade of Sts Peter and Paul's Church on Ulica Grodzka.

One of the statues of the twelve Apostles.

The **interior** has a single nave flanked by intercommunicating chapels. The Jesuit priest and writer, **Piotr Skarga**, author of the *Sermons Preached to the Diet* (1597), is buried in the crypt below the presbytery and a statue to him is located half way along the central aisle. Of particular note in the sumptuous interior is the elaborate *high altar*, an *organ with balustrade* in fine baroque style and the impressive *tomb of Bishop Andrzej Trzebicki*.

The **funerary monument to Andrzej Trzebicki**, bishop of Krakow from 1657 to 1679, is highly spectacular, in keeping with the baroque style enthusiastically adapted from the sumptuous Roman churches during the period of the Counter-Reformation. The monument was made of black marble with limestone statues by his nephew at the end of the 17th century.

Opposite page:
the complex 18th-century structures surrounding the **organ** and the **high altar** are stupendous examples of works based on the designs of Kacper Bażanka, an artist of the late baroque period who trained in Rome; the altar panel representing Christ granting the keys to St Peter, dated 1820 is by Józef Brodowski.

Buried in the crypt is the Jesuit **Piotr Skarga** (1536-1612), author of *Sermons Preached to the Diet* (1597), a political tract published as eight sermons in which he expounds his critical concept of the State and government. As Poland was at the height of its military and territorial power at the time, he was accused of instigating unnecessary unrest by preaching the future downfall of the State. However, after the partition of Poland, the Romantics, and especially Mickiewicz who was a teacher at the Collège de France, considered him to have been a prophet, particularly with reference to an excerpt from the sermons written at the beginning of the 17th century, "All this peace and idleness that you are so fond of will become torment, affliction and wretchedness ... You will find yourselves in the cruel hands of your enemies, who will oppress you more than you oppress your own subjects ....".

The sarcophagus of Andrzej Trzebicki.

X: PIOTR SKARGA PAWĘSKI

The façade of the Franciscan Church; left, the apse in All Saint's Square
(Plac Wszystkich Świętych).

*Opposite, the wall decorations, the late gothic sacred image
of the Mater Dolorosa and below, the Monastery.
Following pages, the stained glass windows by Wyspiański.*

KOŚCIÓŁ FRANCISZKANÓW
The Franciscan Church

The Church and Convent of the Franciscans were built in
1236 and were probably founded by the Silesian Duke Henry
II the Pious for the Franciscans, newly arrived from Prague.
After the terrible fire in Krakow in 1850 the church was restructured in the neo-gothic and neo-romantic styles. Some
elements of the original 13th-century building have survived,
including the frieze on the façade, but many modifications
have been made during various periods. The present decoration of the **interior** dates from the end of
the 19th century and includes some remarkable Art Nouveau fres-
coes on the *walls* of
the transept and pres-
bytery by Stanisław
Wyspiański, who also
made the beautiful
stained glass windows.
The stations of *The
Way of the Cross* are
the work of Józef Me-
hoffer.

THE WALLS AND STAINED GLASS
WINDOWS BY WYSPIAŃSKI

The innovative and impressive wall decorations of
colourful floral designs are in pure Art Nouveau style
were designed by Wyspiański in the late 19th century
The striking series of stained glass windows dedicate
to St Francis, the *Blessed Salome* and the *Four Elements*
(earth, air, fire and water) are deservedly famous, whil
window above the entrance dedicated to *God the Fath*
is considered to be a masterpiece. Stanisław Wyspiańs
(1869-1907) was a painter and dramatist as well as on
of the foremost artists of Polish Modernism and the
national cultural movement, "Young Poland". Complet
documentation of his life and works can be found in th
Wyspiański Museum in Ulica Szczepańska 11.

THE MONASTERY

The Franciscan Monastery and its neighbouring church date from the 13th century; on the walls of the cloister are beautiful gothic frescoes and a gallery of *portraits of Krakow's bishops* in the 16th and 17th centuries.

KAZIMIERZ

This extensive historic district is enclosed by a bend in the river Vistula and became an autonomous city under Casimir III the Great, protected by its own defensive walls. From the 14th century until the Second World War it was home to the Jewish population of Krakow. When the socialist regime came to an end Kazimierz once more began to recover its own particular identity, especially over recent years as many Jewish families have returned permanently, restoring the old buildings and opening new shops, cafes, restaurants, and bookshops.

It is said that Casimir III the Great "found Poland built of wood and left her built of stone" as, during the forty years of his reign (1333-70), he built some fifty castles, founded many cities, twenty-seven of which were surrounded by city walls, and hundreds of villages. An urban settlement that had developed on the banks of the Vistula, which then flowed beneath the present-day Planty Dietla, was raised by Casimir to the status of a city in 1335 and given the name of Kazimierz. In 1796 it was absorbed into the city of Krakow.

Some monuments are evidence of the former autonomy of Kazimierz: the old town hall, **Ratusz kazimierski** in Wolnica Square, remnants of the defensive walls, some churches, including **Kościół Bożego Ciała**, not to mention the name of the street that leads to the Stare Miasto – Ulica Krakowska.

The Jewish Cemetery of Remu'h: the memorial wall, built with fragments of tombstones.

Below, details from the cemetery and ancient sepulchres, including renaissance tombs in white sandstone.

Remu'h Cemetery, The Wailing Wall

STARA BOŻNICA
The Old Synagogue

The Old Synagogue, Stara Bożnica, built at the end of the 14th century at no. 24 Ulica Szeroka, was rebuilt in the 16th century by Matteo Gucci. Entirely renovated after the Second World War, it now houses art and artefacts from the **branch of Muzeum Historyczne Miasta Krakowa** (The Museum of the History of the City of Krakow) and provides an insight into the Jewish religion and culture. The main room in the synagogue is where the faithful congregate to pray and it is here the *bimah* or ornamental cage in wrought iron stands, from which the sentences of the *kahal* are pronounced.

The Jewish community in Poland grew as a result of both the need to escape from persecution in Western Europe, coinciding with Casimir the Great's policy of stimulating the rapid development of cities where shelter could be found, and the favourable reception encouraged by the sovereign. At the outbreak of the Second World War, the Jewish community in Krakow was some 60,000 strong – 23 per cent of the city population. At the time of the closure of the ghetto by the Nazis who had transferred many families there from outside the city, almost 70,000 people were living there. On 13 March 1943 the ghetto was demolished; some of the inhabitants were deported to Płaszów concentration camp while the others were murdered within the confines of the ghetto.

The Old Synagogue: the bimah.

Below, the sacred Ark where the torah *is kept, and an old wall decoration.*

THE HISTORY AND CULTURE OF JEWS IN KRAKOW

This collection of valuable artefacts documenting the religious traditions of the Jews of Krakow, established in 1958, is a section of the Museum of the History of the City of Krakow. Housed on the ground floor of the Old Synagogue – the oldest to have survived in Poland –, the objects on permanent display in the large prayer room relate to the liturgy of the major Jewish festivals.

Some of the most important exhibits are the scroll of the *torah*, read on public occasions and

The Museum of the History and Culture of Jewish Krakow houses valuable old items. Right, Hanukkah menorah (brass, Poland, 2nd half 17th c.).

Left, a crown for the *torah* (Poland, c. 1850).

Below, a ceremonial tray for the Pesach bread with a scene of the Exodus from Egypt (silver, Lvov, c. 1806).

Right, a beautiful silver case for a Book of Esther scroll (Warsaw, 1918-39).

housed in the sacred Ark of the synagogue, the embroidered and silver cases of the *torah* and of the Book of Esther, *menorah*, silver and porcelain dishes for the Pesach bread (the *matzah*), and censers. Photographs and pictures represent traditional men's' and women's' dress, and scenes of everyday life in Kazimierz. The exhibition in the former women's room illustrates moments of family life such as birth, death, marriage, food and religious instruction.

THE JEWISH CEMETERY OF REMU'H AND THE SYNAGOGUE

The Remu'h **Cemetery** dates from 1533 and is one of the most important Jewish cemeteries in Europe. The decorations of the tombs date from various periods and are very interesting. When the historic cemetery was excavated after the war, extremely old and precious tombs were discovered some 60 cm below the surface. They were made of white sandstone from Pińczów and some dated from the 16th century. They were hidden here at the beginning of the 18th century during the Northern War (1703-21). The **Synagogue**, contemporary to the cemetery, is currently one of the most active in Krakow and is named after the philosopher Rabbi Moses Isserles, known as "Remu'h" who lived in the 16th century and is the most famous Polish rabbi.

Above the Remu'h Cemetery and the interior of the Synagogue.

Opposite, above, Remu'h Cemetery.

Discovering Kazimierz

Although one can still sense an air of melancholy, Kazimierz is one of the most fashionable areas of Krakow, offering many bars and cafes as well as cultural entertainment. The Flea Market is an obligatory port of call, and it is well worth visiting the shops selling antiques, old prints, maps, antique books, collections of rare items, and jewelry. There are also many boutiques selling posters which are eagerly collected in Poland.

THE HISTORIC OUTSKIRTS

From the Wawel hill the panorama sweeps towards the western suburbs along the banks of the Vistula, from Zwierzyniec, the district furthest to the west of Krakow, to the ancient Abbey of Tyniec and beyond to the Kościuszko Mound. Following the course of the river through the verdant Las Wolski forests, we arrive at the old Camaldolese hermitage of Bielany.

THE NORBERTINE CONVENT AT ZWIERZYNIEC

One of the medieval suburbs of Krakow was Zwierzyniec (incorporated into the city in 1910), meaning 'hunting reserve' and it is first mentioned in 1224. Here, on the banks of the Vistula stands the **Convent of the Norbertine Nuns** with their **Church** dedicated to St Augustine. It was begun in 1162 in the romanesque style but was destroyed by the Tartars in 1241. Its present appearance is the result of a lengthy series of alterations and additions. In the 18th century the interior was renovated in the neo-classical style. The Norbertine Convent is closely associated with the '*Zwierzyniec horse parade*' or the 'Lajkonik'; held on the first Thursday after Corpus Domini every year this historical celebration has survived since the Middle Ages and is one of the most picturesque folk traditions in Krakow.

Aerial view of the Norbertine Convent at Zwierzyniec.

The **Lajkonik** is a man dressed as a Tartar warrior with a toy horse tied to his belt. He is celebrated in June to commemorate the defeat of the Tartar siege by the citizens of Zwierzyniec in 1287. Dressed in oriental costume, the victorious citizens then made a triumphal entrance to Krakow. The procession in historic costume starts from the monastery and winds its way along the streets to **Rynek Główny**. The celebrations then continue here beneath the Town Hall Tower. The costume now used by Lajkonik was designed in 1904 by Stanisław Wyspiański.

The Kościuszko Mound built by the Polish people in memory of the hero of their own country and of the United States of America.

The equestrian statue of Tadeusz Kościuszko at the entrance to Wawel.

THE KOŚCIUSZKO MOUND

On a hill above the city to the west of Zwierzyniec stands an unusual earth mound covered in grass and surrounded by a circle of brick buildings. The Kościuszko Mound was built between 1821 and 1823 in memory of Tadeusz Kościuszko, a patriot and hero of the battle of Saratoga Springs (1777). The mound in his honour was created by Poles from all over the country bringing handfuls of soil and laying them in his memory. It stands thirty-four metres high and is surmounted by a boulder, brought from the Tatra mountains and inscribed in his memory. The mound contains soil from the battlefields of Poland and America. At the time of the Austrian occupation of Krakow it was surrounded by fortifications. The pyramidal form of the mound dedicated to Tadeusz Kościuszko is in keeping with two other tumuli to the east of the city dateable to the 6th or 7th century. The **Krak Tumulus** and the **Wanda Tumulus** are allegedly the tombs of the founder of Krakow and of his daughter. The Kościuszko mound rises 326 metres above sea-level and affords an excellent panorama of the city and beyond; on a clear day one can see the Tatra mountains, some 100 kms from Krakow. In the 1930s a mound was raised in **memory of Piłsudski** on a nearby hill.

TADEUSZ KOŚCIUSZKO
(Mereszowszczyzna, 1746 – Solothurn, 1817)
A highly talented Polish soldier, a scholar of the military arts, but also of Latin and philosophy, an expert in Polish history, Kościuszko has gone down in history for having lead the resistance movement against the Russians and the Prussians following the second division of Poland (1793). When still a student Kościuszko had lived in Paris (1769) during the years prior to the French revolution and the experience was fundamental in his political development. He was a voluntary soldier in the war of American Independence and, on joining the American army as an engineer, contributed greatly to the their victory at **Saratoga** in 1777, rising to become general of a brigade (1783). On returning to Poland, he organized an uprising against the agreement between Prussia and Russia to divide the Polish nation. The rebel troops gained an important victory at **Racławice** (1794), portrayed in a famous painting by Jan Matejko. However, Kościuszko was defeated at Maciejowice and taken prisoner. After being liberated by Tsar Paul I in 1796, he lived in exile. He is buried in the crypt of St Leonard in Wawel Cathedral.

111

BIELANY

The impressive **Camaldolese Monastery** at Bielany stands on a hill called the Silver Mountain and is perfectly visible from many areas in Krakow. The baroque **interior** of the Bielany church is famous for its 17th-century paintings, especially those by Tommaso Dolabella, a Venetian who became the most celebrated painter in Poland in the first half of the 17th century, working for three kings of the Vasa dynasty. He is best known for his epic works drawing on Polish stylistic tradition, and he had many followers. Just ten minutes drive outside the city the **Las Wolski** forests surrounding the monastery are a traditional spot to enjoy picnics and walks in the summer months.

It is possible to reach Bielany and Tyniec by cruising along the Vistula in boats which leave from Wawel.

TYNIEC

The **Benedictine Abbey** of Tyniec, situated on a limestone hill not unlike Wawel, is one of the oldest monasteries in Poland.

The monastery was already active at the end of the 11th century and the Benedictines were engaged in the painstaking work of copying books and manuscripts. For many centuries the Tyniec Abbey was the main centre for theological studies in Poland. In 1817 it was suppressed and the buildings remained empty until 1939, when the monks returned. In the 1960s as part of the celebrations to mark the millennium of Poland's conversion to Christianity (966-1966)

the monastery sponsored the contemporary translation of the Bible into Polish. The "Millennium Bible" proved to be an excellent translation both for the beauty of its language and for its great theological interest. The abbey church is a basilica with a central nave and single side aisles, with the façade flanked by two massive towers. The splendid baroque interior includes an 18th-century *altar in black marble* (a favourite material at this time) designed by Francesco Placidi (1710-82), an Italian architect who had worked in Dresden before being summoned to Poland by King Augustus III of Saxony in 1742.

THE VISTULA RIVER

The Vistula river, **Wisła**, is the longest in Poland. Rising in the Carpathian mountains it flows for 1047 kilometres, 800 of which are navigable, running cross country, passing Krakow and Warsaw to end in a broad delta in the Gdańsk Bay on the Baltic Sea.

The river enters Krakow beneath the slopes of the Benedictine Abbey at Tyniec. Then flowing just a few meters from St Norbert's Convent at Zwierzyniec runs to the centre of the town where it encircles the hill of Wawel and Kazimierz. It flows away from the city between Nowa Huta and Podgórze. When the weather is fine, a trip in one of the numerous tourist boats offers splendid sights to enjoy from the river.

ENVIRONS

There are many attractive spots to visit in the environs of Krakow.
Places of great historical interest, picturesque villages and parks such as Ojców with the spectacular
Castle of Pieskowa Skała can all be visited on a trip outside the city.

Jan Paweł II
Karol Józef Wojtyła

The Church of the Presentation of the Virgin and the interior showing the baptismal font.

Below, the Birthplace Museum of Karol Wojtyła and the plaque on the façade.

WADOWICE
Birthplace of Pope John Paul II

About fifty kilometres from Krakow, where the river Skawa flows, is the town of Wadowice, founded in the 13th century. The administrative centre for Wadowice county, the town is now renowned as the birthplace of Pope John Paul II. It was here that the former pope received his cultural and spiritual education and today it is an important centre of pilgrimage.

Karol Wojtyła was born on 18 May 1920 at no. 7 Ulica Kościelna, the son of an infantry officer and Emilia Kaczorowska. As a teenager he was a member of Sodality of the Blessed Virgin Mary and developed his acting skills in the school theatre group.

Karol Wojtyła attended both the junior and high school in Wadowice and in 1938 he moved to Krakow to attend the Jagiellonian University.

The Birthplace Museum of John Paul II (**Dom Rodzinny Jana Pawła II**) in Ulica Kościelna no. 7 is of particular interest. The museum documents the most important aspects of Wojtyła's life and work in Poland until becoming pope in 1978. Pictures and documents relating to his earliest childhood are displayed, and in rooms 7 and 8 photographs taken during the 27 years of his papacy are exhibited.

The Cultural Centre (**Dom Kultury**) is situated at Ulica Teatralna 1 in the 19th-century building which housed the "**Sokół**" (Falcon) Gymnastic Society; in the interwar period the Society organised theatrical shows, school performances and physical education lessons in which Karol Wojtyła also participated.

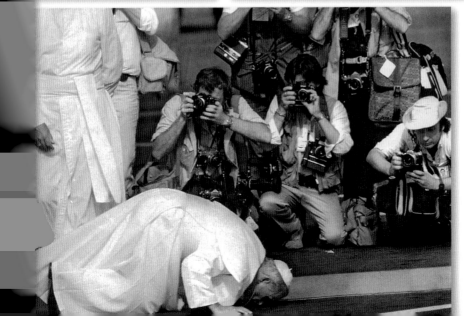

"With filial affection, I embrace the threshold of the home of my birth, giving thanks to divine Providence for the gift of life passed on to me by my beloved parents, for the warmth of the family home, for the love of my dear ones."

John Paul II, Wadowice, 16 June 1999

Pope John Paul II in the early years of his papacy.

The square, now called Plac Jana Pawła II, forms the centre of the town. Facing on to it is the baroque **Bazylika Mniejsza**, the Minor Basilica of the Presentation of the Virgin Mary where Wojtyła came on pilgrimage in 1979, 1991 and 1999 as a homage to the place where he had been baptised and taken his first communion. In 1992 the church received the status of Minor Basilica by papal edict. Of 14th-century origins, the basilica has an attractive gothic baptismal font while the chapel housing the revered image of *Our Lady of Perpetual Help*, crowned by the pope in 1999, is especially important. In 2006 a chapel dedicated to John Paul II was consecrated by pope Benedict XVI.

The Wieliczka mine of rock salt is one o[f] oldest mineral mines in the history of man[.] This ancient mine was included in UNES[CO] First World List of Cultural and Natural Her[itage] in 1978. Only nearby Bochnia is older tha[n] Wieliczka mine, which has been in produ[ction] since the 13th century and is still active. B[elow] ground the complex consists of caverns, [pas]sageways, corridors and lakes with over 30[0] of roads and routes over nine levels from a [depth] of 64 to 327 metres.

This vast deposit of rock salt came into b[eing] 13.5 million years ago when vast deposi[ts of] sea salt crystallised in the Pre-Carpatian b[asin]. Rocky sediments and concretions formed w[ith] continual tectonic shifts transformed into l[ayers] at the lowest level and blocks at higher level[s]. Today rock salt is used for foods and in indu[stry]. In the past it was a vital element for prese[rving] food (so important was it that it was often [used] instead of currency), and under Casimi[r the] Great the industry in Poland was state regul[ated] achieving profits that represented some 3[0 per] cent of the nation's income. The Wieliczka [mine] began to operate in the Middle Ages, introdu[cing] an entirely new way of obtaining salt which [had,] until then, been derived from the evaporatio[n of] saliferous water from salt marshes.

The tourist itinerary covers about 2 km bet[ween] the first and third levels to a depth of 135 m [and] represents the most "historic" area, with e[xten]sive documentation on the evolution of m[ining] techniques.

The visit begins at the **Daniłowicz Shaft** na[med] after the director of the mine from 1635-4[0. The] first chamber on level one is named after **Ni[cho]las Copernicus** who probably saw the mi[ne in] 1493 and was one of the earliest in a long li[ne of] famous personalities to visit, including Wolf[gang] Goethe, Dmitrij Mendeleev, Karol Wojtyła [and] Bill Clinton. In this chamber are the wood [sup]ports used to bear the pressure from the r[oof,] taking advantage of the interaction with the [salt] which hardens the wood and preserves it [for] a long period of time. Of particular intere[st is] the "**Spalone**" (Burnt) **Chamber** where s[ome] centuries ago a fire broke out, destroying [the] wooden props. At a depth of 64 metres is a [sta]tion describing the ancient techniques for m[oni]toring the danger of collapse and gas leaks u[sing] "witnesses" - wooden props which snap u[nder]

1. Janowice Chamber 2. "Spalone"
Chamber 3. Casimir the Great Cham[ber]
with a bust of the king and the Minin[g]
Statute of Krakow commemorative
plaque 4. The Kunegunda Gallery 5,
The Pieskowa Skała Chamber 7. The
Kunegunda Traverse 8. The Holy Cro[ss]
Chapel.

10

11

9. The Chapel of St Kinga *10, 11, 12. The Chapel of St Kinga, with furnishings*

ressure like matchsticks and "penitents", miners who were responsible for burning the methane trapped in the roofs of the chambers as soon as appeared. Also on level one is the **Casimir the Great Chamber**, named for the king who introduced the Mining Statute of Krakow (1368) and the **Kunegunda Traverse** where the extraction of salt from salt marsh water is described, a method that has been used since ancient times. The second level is reached from the highly atmospheric **Pieskowa Skała Chamber**, where an ancient stairway used by the salt bearers is carved into the rock. At the end of this corridor between the upper and lower second level, at a depth between 91.6 and 101.4 metres, is the spectacular **Chapel of St Kinga** (Kunegunda), dedicated to the patron saint of Poland. Created in 1896 in space occupied by an enormous block of green salt, it was furnished during the 20th century with objects made exclusively of salt, including a *monument dedicated to John Paul II*. On the lower second level (100.4 metres deep) is the **Erazm Barącz Chamber** named after the director of the mine from 1917-18, where there is a fascinating small salt lake, while even lower, at 124.7 metres is the **Chamber** dedicated to the geologist **Stanisław Staszic**, where the tourist route reaches its greatest depth.

13. The Weimar Chamber 14. Erazm Barącz Chamber 15. Stanisław Staszic Chamber 16. Józef Piłsudski Chamber and the Piłsudski statue 17. St. John Chapel, 3rd level, at 135 m.

OŚWIĘCIM
AUSCHWITZ

Auschwitz is recognised as symbolising genocide and the Holocaust throughout the entire world. In 1940, almost a year after Hitler's army had invaded Poland, the Nazis created a concentration camp, the Konzentrationlager Auschwitz, using some abandoned buildings in the suburbs of **Oświęcim** – a Polish city annexed to the Third Reich which changed the name to Auschwitz. At first the German occupying forces only used the site to imprison Polish citizens who were believed to be politically dangerous – important members of the resistance and those belonging to political, civil and intellectual circles. Subsequently they were sent to prisons in all the territories under the influence of the Third Reich. The explanation given for this change was the lack of space in Polish prisons, but the creation of the camp was in fact an integral part of the plan for the "Final Solution to the Jewish Question", in other words the elimination of all Jews living under the Reich and territories under its direct influence.

In 1941 the camp was extended when new blocks were built and villages such as Birkenau were annexed. By 1942 Oświęcim-Brzezinka (*Auschwitz-Birkenau*) was the largest camp for the mass extermination of the Jews in Europe. Millions of people died in Auschwitz and the camps at Treblinka, Bełżec, Chełmno and Sobibor.

From 1942 those Jews who were considered unsuitable for hard labour were deported to Auschwitz for immediate death in the gas chambers without distinction of age, sex, or political conviction. Documents reveal that

most of the prisoners were not registered or branded with a number in order to deliberately underestimate the extent of the slaughter. Historians have calculated that from 1940-45 the number of victims of Auschwitz-Birkenau was probably about 1,500,000 people, of whom 1,100,000 were Jews of various nationalities, over 140,000 were Polish (many of whom political prisoners), 20,000 were Gypsies, over 20,000 prisoners of war from various countries (including 10,000 Russians). The majority, Jews deported to Birkenau in 1942, were immediately put to death in the gas chambers on their arrival, while other prisoners died as a result of the inhuman living conditions.

At the end of 1944, the SS began to dismantle the camp, attempting to remove evidence of the massacre. The Red Army liberated Auschwitz on 27 January 1945. An act of the Polish parliament on 2 July 1947 established the **Państwowe Muzeum Auschwitz-Birkenau** (National Museum to the memory of the victims of Auschwitz-Birkenau), located on the 191 hectares which housed the ruins of the prison blocks, the gas chambers, the crematoria, the rail link between Auschwitz and Birkenau and the **Judenrampe** where, between 1942 and 1944 Jews prisoners destined for Birkenau were selected. For many years the International Auschwitz Committee, consisting of many ex-prisoners of various nations, has been responsible for organising exhibitions in memory of the victims of the Holocaust.

PIESKOWA SKAŁA

The Vistula, flowing through Krakow from west to east, divides the Carpathian foothills, to the south of the city, from the Jurassic limestone cliffs of Krakowsko-Częstochowska Highland. Between 1333 and 1346 Casimir the Great built a chain of fortresses on the rocky peaks on the border with Silesia to defend Poland against attacks by John of Luxembourg. Known as "eagles' nests" these fortresses were so built as to enable each one to communicate with its two neighbours by means of flares. The **fortress** of Pieskowa Skała was positioned between Ojców, which passed on communications to Wawel, and those castles further to the north.

Some 25 km from Krakow, Pieskowa is often called the "Little Wawel" for its renaissance courtyard modelled on the one at Wawel. The position of the Pieskowa Skała fortress was of the greatest strategic importance: it is built on a rocky peak with sheer drops from three sides of its walls.

The castle houses two exhibitions: one devoted to the *History of the Pieskowa Skała Castle* and the other to *Stylistic changes in European Art from the Middle Ages to the first half of the Eighteenth Century.* The restaurant in one of the towers affords fine views of the terrace and the formal garden beyond the castle walls.

An aerial view of the Castle of Pieskowa Skała, known as a "pearl of the Polish Renaissance".

Opposite: Morskie Oko (The Eye of the Sea) Lake and Mieguszowieckie Peaks.

THE TATRAS

Lying mainly in Slovakia and forming the natural border between Poland and Slovakia, the Tatras are the highest mountain chain of the Carpathians. The highest mountains are the *Rysy* in Poland at 2499 metres and *Gerlachovský štít* reaching 2655 metres in Slovakia. The Tatras – "the Polish Alps" – are also the only mountains with an Alpine formation in Central Europe and their structure is highly varied: the rocky peaks are of granite, limestone has formed an area of many caves, while the forests and mountain pastures are pleasantly verdant and the highest peaks are tundra-like. The fauna includes rare animals such as the lynx, brown bears, eagles and Alpine chamois. The **Tatras National Park** is responsible for maintaining this wonderful natural heritage. The Tatras mountains are also renowned for winter sports and Zakopane is the Polish "Winter Capital" of all the ski resorts. With some 50 ski-lifts, slopes for all abilities and various levels of difficulty, this is not only the best known but also best equipped resort and numerous competitions are held here.

CONTENTS